Dispatch Seminar

2020 Edition

plus

The Dispatch Manual and The Successful Truck Owner Operator

A Comprehensive Resource and Instructions Manual for the Entrepreneur Starting a Home Based Business Dispatch Service

Published By TruckingSuccess.com

Copyright © 2020 – TruckingSuccess.com – All rights reserved.
Reproduction in any manner, in whole or in part, without permission is prohibited.

Table of Contents Truck Dispatch Seminar

Introduction
Chapter 1 – Truck & Trailer
Chapter 2 – Your Home Office
Chapter 3 – Getting to Know Your Client
Chapter 4 – Setting Up A Client Account
Chapter 5 – Setting Up A Client File and Organize the Client Documents.
Chapter 6 – How to Work with Brokerage Companies
Chapter 7 – How to find Loads and what Load Board to Use

Table of Contents Dispatch Manual

Introduction
Chapter 1 – Transportation Industry Overview
Chapter 2 – Tools Of The Trade
Chapter 3 – Professionalism
Chapter 4 – Load Availability
Chapter 5 – Finding the Right Loads
Chapter 6 – Booking Loads
Chapter 7 – Freight Handling
Chapter 8 – Freight Delivery

Table of Contents The Successful Truck Owner Operator

Chapter 1 Getting Started
Economic Outlook New HOS Regulations CSA 2010
Commercial Drivers License
Chapter 2 Business Structures
Sole Proprietorship Partnership Corporations / LLC
Chapter 3 Buying your Truck
Financial Aspects Selecting a Used Truck Maintenance & Repair
Chapter 4 Operating Authority
Leasing On Negotiating a Lease Own Authority
Chapter 5 Business Records
Maintaining Records Cash Management- Cost-Per-Mile Calculation
Chapter 6 Registration & Taxes
Vehicle Registration Fuel & Road Taxes Log Book – Trip Sheet ELD Regulations

Dispatch Seminar

The seminar teaches the entrepreneur planning to start a dispatch service business how to set up a business and succeed in a new venture.

Before we proceed to each chapter please get yourself familiar with several useful informative details about setting up a home based business. Go to: https://www.truckingsuccess.com/home-based-business

Chapter 1 - Truck & Trailer - If you have no experience in regards to the trucking industry, this chapter will explain some truck & trailer parts. Functions you need to get yourself familiar with, in order to communicate professionally with your clients.

Tractor/trailer (18 wheeler)

The front wheels of a tractor are referred to as "the steering" When a tractor/trailer is completely loaded, the maximum amount of pounds allowed by law is 80,000 pounds. These pounds have to be split to several axels. The steering wheels (first axel) are allowed to carry 12,000 pounds.

The two axels with 8 tires behind the cab are referred to as "the drives". The drives are allowed to carry 34,000 pounds.

The two axels at the end of the trailer are referred to as "rear end" and they are also allowed by law to carry 34,000 pounds.

Since a trucker can't instruct the loading personnel to load his trailer exactly the way explained above, he has to make sure that he is not overloading on any of the axels. Most loads are not maxed out to 80,000 pounds, therefore he has plenty of opportunity to move his trailer tandem and also move his 5th wheel to place the exact amount of pounds on each axel allowed by law. The dispatcher is of course not responsible when a client is over loading the truck, therefore, the dispatcher should only book loads with a brokerage company, which do not accede the amount of pounds allowed by law.

Example: Your clients tractor weighs 16,000 pounds and the trailer weighs 14,000 pounds. The unit therefore weighs empty 30,000 pounds. Since you know now that the maximum allowed is 80,000 pounds, you can only book loads with a brokerage company up to 50,000 pounds. However, truckers don't like to be loaded up to the maximum, you should always look for loads under 50,000 pounds.

Chapter 2 - Your Home Office.

No matter where you live, house or apartment, you need to separate your business from all other family activities around you. Creating a small office in one of the rooms is always the best way to go. You need to be totally concentrated on the job when you deal with your clients livelihood. They rely on your ability to find the best paying loads available. You need to set up the following equipment:

1. Phone landline plus a separate cell phone in order to be available for your clients all the time. Dispatching is not a 3-5 hour job, you need to be accessible 24 hours a day. Please understand, you don't have to work all these hours. Most dispatching is done between 8 AM and 1 PM.

However, in order to keep a client on board, you have to let them know that you always available if they need help in case of an emergency.

2. PC computer or laptop

3. Printer, Scan and fax - Most printers have all 3 functions. You do not need a fax these days because most brokerage companies will accept scans for the forms, bill of lading, rate confirmation sheet, invoices etc.

3. Download adobe acrobat reader software for PDF documents. If you like to sign documents as a electronic signature, you need to purchase the adobe acrobat professional version.

4. Set up a company name for your operation and maybe file a LLC corporation with your state corporation commission.

5. Purchase a domain name, related with your company name and create a professional email address for your business.

6. Create a small website for internet marketing and SEO purposes. Also for marketing purposes create a small video, outlining your services, and place it on YouTube.

7. Advertise your services on all social media you can think of, like Face Book, Twitter, Instagram etc.

8. In order to promote your business, you also need to place free classified ads all over the internet. There are thousands of sites available, please spent at least one hour per day and place these ads, you need exposure in the beginning because starting a new business is always a job only for the person who is consistent in order to succeed.

Chapter 3 - Getting to know your client.

You need to get an understanding for the truck drivers daily struggle on American Highways. In other words, you must learn to handle his personality and after some time you should be able to read his mind. Know what kind of loads he like to haul and when he wants to go home. In the first two to three weeks you need to communicate with him more often because you need to create a relationship, get to know him and get him to feel comfortable with your services. The relationship should have a pleasant understanding because the client is your income and you like to keep them on board. Remember, your business depends on a recurrent income.

You need to know how many miles they can drive per day. This information will help you booking loads, that can be delivered on time. If he/she can't make the delivery on time, you have to reject that load and search for another load.

Information: A truck driver can drive behind the wheels for 11 hours and he also got 3 hours of no driving time. This time is reserved for unloading or other business related activities. After 14 hours on the job he is required by law to spend 10 hours in the sleeper. After 5 days on the job (5 X 14 hours) he is required after 70 hours at work, to spend 34 hours off time before he can get back to the job and start driving.

Chapter 4 - Setting up a clients account.

Tell your client, that you need 4-5 days to set up his account. Inform him that your monthly flat fee is $450.00 and handling extra paperwork (invoicing & payment routing etc.) you charge an additional $45.00 per month. Explain to him that you can't charge a percentage of the loads, because you are not a brokerage company. You don't have a broker's license. You don't carry a $75,000 bond, you don't carry insurance and you may be subject to all kinds of lawsuits when things go wrong. However, if your client agrees with a percentage of the load, you need to place the authorization into your contract. Let him/her know that you have set up your business legally and that you work ethical correct inside the industry.

Ask, how you should handle the schedule, in other words, how many days they would like to stay out and how many times per month they want to be home with the family. Also ask in what area of the United States they would like to operate.

Explain that you need a short contract between the two parties because you are signing documents on their behalf and you need the authorization to do that.

You also let the client know that you sent an email with an attachment for the contract and inform them, what kind of documentation you need in order to set up the account.

The following includes a sample of the email, the contract between the parties and sample forms you will receive from your client:

A: Email letter to Client:

Subject: Your company name - Dispatch Service

Hello Mr. or Mrs. (customer name)
Please find as an attachment to this email the contract between our two companies. The reason for the contract is the simple fact, that I have to sign brokerage contracts and rate confirmation sheets on your behalf. Most brokerage companies these days don't accept any signature signed by an independent dispatcher. That is absolutely understandable since in the past a lot of these so called dispatchers have double or triple brokered loads and signed illegally their contracts. If you have any questions about that matter, please don't hesitate and call me at: (phone number)
In order to set up your account (no set up fees) please return via scan or fax (fax number) the following documents:
- Signed contract between our companies
- MC authority certificate
- Insurance certificate
- Copy of your driver's license (both sides)
- Medical examiners certificate
- Your W9 form

- Your truck & trailer number
- A list of at least 3 brokerage companies you have already done business with

Thank you very much for your interest in my services, if you have any questions please call me at: (phone number)

Best regards,
Your name your phone number your fax number

P.S. You need these certificates and forms from your clients because the brokerage company requests these documents before you can book a load with them. Once you are set up with an account, you don't need to sent the documents again. It is a one-time effort on your part to set up an account and become a customer with the brokerage company on behalf of your client.

If you have any questions after you studied the seminar, you can call us any time for 30 days after your purchase and get additional questions you may have, answered.

B: Sample Contract to Client:

Tiffiny's Dispatch Solutions
13700 ABC Circle, ABC Grove, CA 92843
Phone: 714-468-0000 Fax: 714-000-0000
Email: ABC@gmail.com

DISPATCH SERVICE AGREEMENT

This Dispatch Service Agreement is entered into this day   of , between the following parties whose names and addresses are set forth below:

ABC Express
3675 Brookwood Blvd
Rex, GA 30273

and

Tiffiny's Dispatch Solutions
137 ABC Circle
ABC Grove, CA 92843

The above parties hereby agree that upon the commencement date of this Dispatch Service Agreement, both parties are bound by the terms of this Agreement.

This Agreement shall not be changed, modified, or rescinded except in writing and any attempt at oral modification of this agreement shall be void.
The purposes, terms and conditions of this Dispatch Service Agreement are as follows:

PURPOSE

Tiffiny's Dispatch Solutions will provide a transportation dispatch service to ABC Express during the duration of this Agreement. The scope of this service is limited to finding, providing and dispatching loads on behalf of ABC Express.

TERMS

ABC Express will provide in a timely manner to Tiffiny's Dispatch Solutions the following information needed for dispatch:

Date and time when truck will be available for dispatch.
Location of truck to be dispatched.
Preferred destination for truck to be dispatched to.
Alternative destination for truck to be dispatched to.
Estimate of expected freight rate/revenue of requested load.

Tiffiny's Dispatch Solutions will locate loads based on the aforementioned criteria on behalf of ABC Express and will provide the load information to ABC Express.

ABC Express is not obligated to accept the load(s) located by Tiffiny's Dispatch Solutions. However, once ABC Express has accepted the load(s), ABC Express will assume all responsibilities for the load(s), including picking up and delivering the dispatched load(s). ABC Express will also carry liability insurance in the amount of 1 million dollars and cargo insurance in the amount of $100,000.00.

ABC Express authorizes Tiffiny's Dispatch Solutions to sign contracts with brokers and shippers on behalf of ABC Express. ABC Express agrees to honor all non-competitive clauses as set forth in the transportation contracts and agreements of brokers and shippers which Tiffiny's Dispatch Solutions signs on behalf of ABC Express.

CONDITIONS

Tiffiny's Dispatch Solutions charges a monthly fee of $450.00 per truck (Four Hundred fifty) for the load dispatch service, which is due on the first day of each month. The initial monthly service fee of $450.00 will be pro-rated and is due and payable by credit card after this Agreement is signed and returned to Tiffiny's Dispatch Solutions.

The term of this Agreement is from month to month unless canceled. Either party can cancel this Agreement at any time giving notice at least 1 week before the end of the month.
The parties understand and agree that:

* Tiffiny's Dispatch Solutions is not a freight broker and does not act as one.
* Tiffiny's Dispatch Solutions does not receive commissions from shippers or brokers who originated the loads.
* Tiffiny's Dispatch Solutions has no financial interest in the loads dispatched and is not responsible for the settlement of loads dispatched.
* ABC Express is solely and exclusively responsible for billing and collecting payments for the dispatched loads that ABC

Express accepted and agreed to deliver. Other arrangements can be negotiated.

IN WITNESS WHEREOF, the parties hereto have signed this Dispatch Service Agreement on the day and year first written above.

ABC Express   Tiffiny's Dispatch Solutions

C: Forms you receive from your clients

MC Authority Certificate

U.S. Department of Transportation
Federal Motor Carrier Safety Administration

400 7th Street SW
Washington, DC 20590

SERVICE DATE
March 15, 2006

DECISION
MC-552839

D/B/A B & B TRANSPORT
CHILOQUIN, OR
REENTITLED

On March 9, 2006, applicant filed a request to have the Federal Motor Carrier Safety Administration's records changed to reflect a name change.

It is ordered:
The Federal Motor Carrier Safety Administration's records are amended to reflect the carrier's name as WILLIAM F BAILEY, D/B/A B & B TRANSPORTATION.

Within 30 days after this decision is served, the applicant must establish that it is in full compliance with the statute and the insurance regulations by having amended filings on prescribed FMCSA forms (BMC91 or 91X or 82 for bodily injury and property damage liability, BMC 34 or 83 for cargo liability, or a BMC 84 or 85 for property broker security and BOC-3 for designation of agents upon whom process may be served) submitted on its behalf. Copies of Form MCS-90 or other "certificates of insurance" are not acceptable evidence of insurance compliance. Insurance and BOC-3 filings should be sent to Federal Motor Carrier Safety Administration, 400 Virginia Avenue, SW, Suite 600, Washington, DC 20024.

The applicant is notified that failure to comply with the terms of this decision shall result in revocation of its operating rights registration, effective 30 days from the service date of this decision.

To verify that the applicant is in full compliance, call (202)358-7000 or visit our web site at: http://li-public.fmcsa.dot.gov. Any other questions regarding the action taken should be directed to (202)366-9805.

Decided: March 10, 2006
By the Federal Motor Carrier Safety Administration

Angeli Sebastian, Chief
Information Systems Division

NC/A

Insurance Certificate

ACORD CERTIFICATE OF LIABILITY INSURANCE

DATE (MM/DD/YYYY): 01/03/2007

PRODUCER Phone: (209) 474-2771 Fax: (209) 474-0216
G M LAWRENCE INSURANCE BROKERAGE
7746 LORRAINE AVENUE SUITE 214
STOCKTON CA 95210

Agency Lic#: 0522491

THIS CERTIFICATE IS ISSUED AS A MATTER OF INFORMATION ONLY AND CONFERS NO RIGHTS UPON THE CERTIFICATE HOLDER. THIS CERTIFICATE DOES NOT AMEND, EXTEND OR ALTER THE COVERAGE AFFORDED BY THE POLICIES BELOW.

INSURERS AFFORDING COVERAGE — NAIC #

INSURED
DBA ███ TRANSPORTATION
6510 S 6TH ST #28
KLAMATH FALLS OR 97603

- INSURER A: LANCER INSURANCE COMPANY
- INSURER B:
- INSURER C:
- INSURER D:
- INSURER E:

COVERAGES

THE POLICIES OF INSURANCE LISTED BELOW HAVE BEEN ISSUED TO THE INSURED NAMED ABOVE FOR THE POLICY PERIOD INDICATED. NOTWITHSTANDING ANY REQUIREMENT, TERM OR CONDITION OF ANY CONTRACT OR OTHER DOCUMENT WITH RESPECT TO WHICH THIS CERTIFICATE MAY BE ISSUED OR MAY PERTAIN, THE INSURANCE AFFORDED BY THE POLICIES DESCRIBED HEREIN IS SUBJECT TO ALL THE TERMS, EXCLUSIONS AND CONDITIONS OF SUCH POLICIES. AGGREGATE LIMITS SHOWN MAY HAVE BEEN REDUCED BY PAID CLAIMS.

INSR LTR	ADD'L INSRD	TYPE OF INSURANCE	POLICY NUMBER	POLICY EFFECTIVE DATE (MM/DD/YY)	POLICY EXPIRATION DATE (MM/DD/YY)	LIMITS	
		GENERAL LIABILITY				EACH OCCURRENCE	$
		☐ COMMERCIAL GENERAL LIABILITY				DAMAGE TO RENTED PREMISES (Ea occurrence)	$
		☐ CLAIMS MADE ☐ OCCUR				MED. EXP (Any one person)	$
						PERSONAL & ADV INJURY	$
						GENERAL AGGREGATE	$
		GEN'L AGGREGATE LIMIT APPLIES PER: ☐ POLICY ☐ PROJECT ☐ LOC				PRODUCTS-COMP/OP AGG.	$
A		**AUTOMOBILE LIABILITY** ☐ ANY AUTO ☐ ALL OWNED AUTOS ☒ SCHEDULED AUTOS ☐ HIRED AUTOS ☐ NON-OWNED AUTOS	CM0043588-00	12/17/06	12/17/07	COMBINED SINGLE LIMIT (Ea accident)	$ 1,000,000
						BODILY INJURY (Per person)	$
						BODILY INJURY (Per accident)	$
						PROPERTY DAMAGE (Per accident)	$
		GARAGE LIABILITY ☐ ANY AUTO				AUTO ONLY - EA ACCIDENT	$
						OTHER THAN AUTO ONLY: EA ACC / AGG	$
		EXCESS / UMBRELLA LIABILITY ☐ OCCUR ☐ CLAIMS MADE				EACH OCCURRENCE	$
						AGGREGATE	$
		☐ DEDUCTIBLE ☐ RETENTION $					$
		WORKERS COMPENSATION AND EMPLOYERS' LIABILITY ANY PROPRIETOR/PARTNER/EXECUTIVE OFFICER/MEMBER EXCLUDED? If yes, describe under SPECIAL PROVISIONS below				WC STATUTORY LIMITS / OTHER	
						E.L. EACH ACCIDENT	$
						E.L. DISEASE-EA EMPLOYEE	$
						E.L. DISEASE-POLICY LIMIT	$
B		OTHER: MOTOR TRUCK CARGO	CM0043588-00	12/17/06	12/17/07	$100,000.00 PER VEHICLE $1000.00 DEDUCTIBLE INCLUDING REEFER BREAKDOWN	

DESCRIPTION OF OPERATIONS/LOCATIONS/VEHICLES/EXCLUSIONS ADDED BY ENDORSEMENT/ SPECIAL PROVISIONS
1998 INTERNATIONAL TRACTOR #2HSFHASR1WC044428, 2000 UTILITY TRAILER #1UYVS2538YU060404

THIS CERTIFICATE IS INVALID IF SENT TO OTHER CERTIFICATE HOLDERS

CERTIFICATE HOLDER

Attention:

CANCELLATION

SHOULD ANY OF THE ABOVE DESCRIBED POLICIES BE CANCELLED BEFORE THE EXPIRATION DATE THEREOF, THE ISSUING INSURER WILL ENDEAVOR TO MAIL 30 DAYS WRITTEN NOTICE TO THE CERTIFICATE HOLDER NAMED TO THE LEFT, BUT FAILURE TO DO SO SHALL IMPOSE NO OBLIGATION OR LIABILITY OF ANY KIND UPON THE INSURER, IT'S AGENTS OR REPRESENTATIVES.

AUTHORIZED REPRESENTATIVE

ACORD 25 (2001/08)   Certificate # 281   © ACORD CORPORATION 1988

W9 Form

Form W-9 (Rev. January 2002)
Department of the Treasury
Internal Revenue Service

Request for Taxpayer Identification Number and Certification

Give form to the requester. Do not send to the IRS.

Name: WILLIAM F. ▓▓▓

Business name, if different from above: ▓▓ TRANSPORTATION

Check appropriate box: ☒ Individual/Sole proprietor ☐ Corporation ☐ Partnership ☐ Other ▶ .... ☐ Exempt from backup withholding

Address (number, street, and apt. or suite no.): P.O. BOX 4

City, state, and ZIP code: SPRAGUE RIVER OR. 97639

Requester's name and address (optional):

List account number(s) here (optional):

Part I — Taxpayer Identification Number (TIN)

Social security number: _ _ _ – _ _ – _ _ _ _

or

Employer identification number: 20-2141 6019

Part II — Certification

Under penalties of perjury, I certify that:

1. The number shown on this form is my correct taxpayer identification number (or I am waiting for a number to be issued to me), and
2. I am not subject to backup withholding because: (a) I am exempt from backup withholding, or (b) I have not been notified by the Internal Revenue Service (IRS) that I am subject to backup withholding as a result of a failure to report all interest or dividends, or (c) the IRS has notified me that I am no longer subject to backup withholding, and
3. I am a U.S. person (including a U.S. resident alien).

Sign Here — Signature of U.S. person ▶ Wm Bailey   Date ▶ 4-10-06

Chapter 5 - Setting up a client file and organize your clients documents.

You have to create a client file folder with pouches inside. On the left side you will organize all your clients documents. (see letter to client)

On the right side you will organize the paperwork you receive from the brokerage company including the brokerage contract etc. The documents you receive from the brokerage company will be explained after this chapter.

You need to place a sticker on the front of your file with all your clients information. This information should include the following:

1. Carrier name, 2. carrier address, 3. drivers name, 4. MC #, 5. drivers cell phone, 6. drivers home phone, 7. drivers fax #, 8. truck #, 9. trailer #, 10. VIN #, 11. empty weight, 12. DOT #, 13 insurance phone #, 14. EIN #.

Chapter 6 - How to work with brokerage companies.

You must establish a good business relationship with each brokerage company. It will take some time, but always remember, the best paying loads always go to the carrier, the broker did business with and the carrier they are doing business with for some time.

If you contact a brokerage company on behalf of your client for the first time, the experience might be quite different from another brokerage company you're calling. One company might have done business with your client before, and all his credentials are on file, therefore all the brokerage company will sent over to you, is the rate confirmation sheet. You have to sign the rate confirmation sheet, and sent it back to the company and the load is yours. All you have to do now, forward the rate confirmation sheet to your client so he/she got all the information necessary to pick up the load. Example of the rate confirmation sheet bext page:

02/26/2007 14:01   74032263847403226384   FLEET SERVICE INC   PAGE 01

02/26/07 2:11 PM

Fleet Service Inc.
P.O. BOX 4070   NEWARK, OH 43058-4070
PH# 800-999-7566   FAX # 740-322-6384

CONFIRMATION & FREIGHT MOVEMENT RECORD AGREEMENT

CARRIER: B & B TRANSPORTATION
CARRIER CODE: BBTSPR
PHONE#   (602)864-8056
FAX#   (602)864-2922   ATTN:JW ____JW.____

LOAD AT: DEL TO:
YENKIN MAJESTIC   PNS/MACFRUGALS DC - BIG LOTS DC
1100 Woodland Ave.   12434 4th Street
Columbus, OH   RANCHO CUCAMONGA, CA
43219   91730
[LOAD TIME: 3/5/2007 7:30:00 AM   DEL TIME: 3/9/2007 6:00:00 AM

P/U #: 73055   APPT #:   701163
P/O #: ~~73058~~ 4110735

EXTRA PICKUPS / STOPS:

PHONE #   DATE: Revised → || Reefer ||
                                                       50°
TRUCK PAY:

FLAT RATE: $ 2500.00
               ~~$200~~   Reefer $200.00
TOTAL: $ 2700.00 ← Total

MUST BE ON TIME! ALL DRIVERS MUST CALL WHEN EMPTY FOR RELEASE NUMBER

Accepts this load according to the conditions above.
Mail signed Bill of Lading to Fleet Service, P.O. 4070, Newark, Ohio 43058
1. Carrier Invoice with Load # __71614__ and original signed Bill of Lading
2. Carrier, Sign and fax this form to 740-322-6384 asap
3. Carrier must call Fleet Service when shipment is loaded with B/L#, Pcs, and Weight
   (Failure to call within 24 hours of loading will result in $100.00 penalty per day)
4. Driver is responsible for counting material before signing bill of lading. If you are picking up material that is "shrink wrapped when driver arrived," sign only for number of pallets. Trailers are to be sealed and "shipper note seal number of bills." Receiver must mark seal intact on arrival

DATE: 2-26-07   Carrier Signature: _JW. [signature]_
DATE: 2/26/07   Fleet Signature: _Vicky_

DRIVER TO CALL 800-999-7566 FOR DISPATCH AND DIRECTIONS.
THANK YOU FOR USING FLEET SERVICE, INC.

If you call a brokerage company and this company did not do any business with your client before, you have to handle quite some paperwork in order to secure the load. Remember that this will be a one-time process because after you have exchanged all the paperwork required, you don't have to do again. The process will start as follows:

First, the brokerage company will sent you a so called package. This package will include the following documents:

1. Brokerage contract between your client and the brokerage company. You will sign this contract on behalf of your client. (remember, you need a client contract between you and your client)

2. Brokerage MC # (brokerage companies also carry a MC #)

3. Brokerage Insurance certificate

4. Brokerage Bond certificate of $75,000

5. Brokerage W 9 form

Second, when you receive the package, sign the brokerage contract immediately, add your clients documents, MC #, insurance certificate, W9 form, drivers license and medical certificate, truck & trailer # and also the reference list and sent it back. Time is of the essence because the load you want might be gone after some time, because another agent inside the brokerage company handed it over to another carrier. Don't be encouraged, at least you are now signed up and another load might be available from the same brokerage company after all your documents are excepted. Some brokerage companies have now a complete sign-up on-line, all they need, is your clients insurance certificate. All you have to do, follow the instructions on-line.

If your client ask you to handle his paperwork to get paid, you need to ask what kind of pay period he would like. Brokerage companies pay in 30 days or they offer quick pay. If your client need quick pay, ask the brokerage company what percentage they are charging. Most companies charge between 1.5 and 3 % from the rate of the load. Example: If the load pays $3,000 and the company charges 3%, you need to deduct $90.00 from your invoice. The amount the brokerage company will wire into your clients bank account is $2,910.00.

If you handle your clients paperwork, the following documents need to be sent to the brokerage company a.s.a.p. because they pay in 2 business days.

1. Bill of lading (signed)

2. Rate confirmation sheet

3. Invoice.

See samples of the bill of lading and invoice next pages::

STRAIGHT BILL OF LADING – ORIGINAL – NOT NEGOTIABLE

Shipper's No. _____

Carrier _____ SCAC _____ Carrier's No. _____

RECEIVED, subject to individually determined rates or contracts that have been agreed upon in writing between the carrier and shipper, if applicable, otherwise to the rates, classifications and rules that have been established by the carrier and are available to the shipper, on request; and all applicable state and federal regulations;

at _____ date _____ from _____

the Property described below, in apparent good order, except as noted (contents and condition of contents of packages unknown, marked, consigned, and destined as indicated below which said company (the word company being understood throughout this contract as meaning any person or corporation in possession of the property under the contract) agrees to carry to delivery at said destination, if on its route, or otherwise to deliver to another carrier on the route to said destination. It is mutually agreed as to each carrier of all or any of said Property over all or any portion of said route to destination and as to each party at any time interested in all or any of said Property that every service to be performed hereunder shall be subject to all the conditions not prohibited by law, whether printed or written, herein contained, including the conditions on the back hereof, which are hereby agreed to by the shipper and accepted for himself and his assigns.

Consigned to _____

Destination	State	County	Zip	Delivery Address

Route _____

Delivering Carrier _____   **Vehicle Number** _____

Number of Packages	Description of Articles	Weight (sub. to correction)	Class or Rate	
				Subject to Section 7 of conditions, if shipment is to be delivered to the consignee without recourse on the consignor, the consignor shall sign the following statement: The carrier shall not make delivery of shipment without payment of freight and all other lawful charges.
				(Signature of Consignor)
				FREIGHT CHARGES:
				Prepaid ☐
				Collect ☐
				COD AMT: $ _____
				TOTAL CHARGES:

Collect On Delivery and remit to	COD FEE:	Prepaid ☐	$ _____
$	$	Collect ☐	

NOTE: Where the rate is dependent on value, shippers are required to state specifically in writing the agreed or declared value of the property. The agreed declared value of the property is hereby specifically stated by the shipper to be not exceeding $ _____ per _____

NOTE: Liability Limitation for loss or damage in this shipment may be applicable. See 49 U.S.C. 14706(c)(1)(A) and (B).

Shipper: _____ Carrier: _____

Per: _____ Date: _____ Per: _____ Date: _____

201-BLC-Q 3 12462

Adrian's Transport Inc.

INVOICE

Invoice #: 133
Invoice Date: 5/9/2018

Bill To:
Reynolds Logistics, Inc.
PO Box 46166
Plymouth, MN 55446

Ship To:
Reynolds Logistics, Inc.
PO Box 46166
Plymouth, MN 55446

Date	Your Order #	Our Order #	Sales Rep.	FOB	Ship Via	Terms	Tax ID
9-21-2017	0205035	n/a	Brad Fifield	n/a	truck	10 days	82-1786538

Quantity	Item	Units	Description	Discount %	Taxable	Unit Price	Total
1	n/a	1	Food Products	n/a	n/a	985.00	985.00
			From Vernon, CA				
			To Gridley, CA				
			10 day quick pay 2%			19.70	- 19.70
						Subtotal	965.30
						Tax	n/a
						Miscellaneous	n/a
						Balance Due	965.30

REMITTANCE
Please transfer funds electronically to:
Adrian's Transport Inc.
Bank of America
Routing # 121000000
Bank Account # 325069590000

Adrian's Transport Inc., 25740 Abc Canyon Road, Riverside, CA 92584
Phone: (602) 864-8056 or (951) 566-6000 E-mail: wlessing@cox.net or abcdedoval82@yahoo.com

Chapter 7 - How to find loads and what load board to use.

We are recommending the use of the DAT load board. It is the oldest load board in the United States and now it is also the biggest load board. DAT has just purchased Get Loaded.com. The load board is also the safest board on the market today, because DAT will only allow brokerage firms with a 90+ credit rating onto the board.

What does that mean for you? You never have to be afraid that some brokerage companies will not pay and your client never will see his money. That would be of course devastating to your clients business, as well as your business and your reputation. The board also will tell you if a company is a member of the TIA, the oldest organization who keeps track of all brokerage companies and allows only companies with the highest ethical standards to become members of the organization. Bottom line, you are playing it safe from the start.

The use of the load board is pretty easy to navigate and you can sign up on our website https://www.truckingsuccess.com.

You can find loads by navigating in a certain radius where your truck is located at the time and you can also narrow it down to the destination you want to go. You also can place your clients truck in advance at the destination he wants to go.

Always use advance dispatching. You know that your client wants to go out on Monday morning, you do not start looking for loads on Monday morning. You start already looking for the Monday load at least 3-5 days in advance. When your client leaves the loading place on Monday morning, you already start looking for a load at his/her destination, even if it takes him 3 days to get there. Always in advance, never let him sit in a truck stop with no load waiting for him. Always remember, when his wheels are not rolling, he is making no money. He/she will look soon for another dispatcher.

If your client is hauling in 48 States, please use the round trip concept.

Example: loads from the west coast to the east coast paying a decent mileage rate. Loads from the east coast to the west coast are paying, let's say very badly. That's when the round trip concept makes absolutely sense. You need to book a load from the east coast to the mid west and then go from the mid west back to the west coast.

Example: load from west coast to east coast pays $6,000.00 - load from east coast to mid west $1,000.00 - load from mid west to west coast pays $3,600.00 - Round trip total: $10,600.00

If you would have taken a load from the east coast back to the west coast for $3,600.00 your round trip would be $9,600.00. With the round trip concept you gained $1,000.00 more for your client.

Below please find some screen shots from the DAT load board.

Remember, if you have any questions, please call us any time for 30 days after your purchased the dispatch seminar. Call 602-864-8056

Screen shots DAT load board:

	Pro (Best Value)	Enhanced	Standard
	$99.95 / Month 30 days free SIGN UP NOW	$49.95 / Month 30 days free SIGN UP NOW	$34.95 / Month 30 days free SIGN UP NOW
Unlimited Truck Posts — Post your trucks. FREE.	✓	✓	✓
Unlimited Load Searches — Find the best loads fast.	✓	✓	✓
Alarm Match Notification — Get an alert when a new load matches what you're looking for.	✓	✓	✓
Easy Month-to-Month Billing — Low monthly fee, no long term contract.	✓	✓	✓
Mileage & Routing — Optimize your route with mapping services.	✓	✓	✓
Weather & Road Conditions — Get the latest forecasts for the U.S. & Canada.	✓	✓	✓
Broker Days-to-Pay Score — On average, our brokers pay within 28 days.	✓	✓	
Broker Credit Profiles — On average, our brokers have credit scores of 94 or above out of 100.	✓	✓	
Phone Posting and Searching — Post & search on the road, without a laptop.	✓	✓	
Broker Spot Market Lane Rates — See the average rates for lanes you're searching.	✓	✓	
NEW! 15-day Lane Rates — Get fresh Broker-to-carrier spot market lane rates	✓		
Triangle Haul — Get automatic TriHaul routing suggestions	✓		
Single lane rate lookups — Access DAT RateView for any lookup	✓		
Access to the North American database	✓		

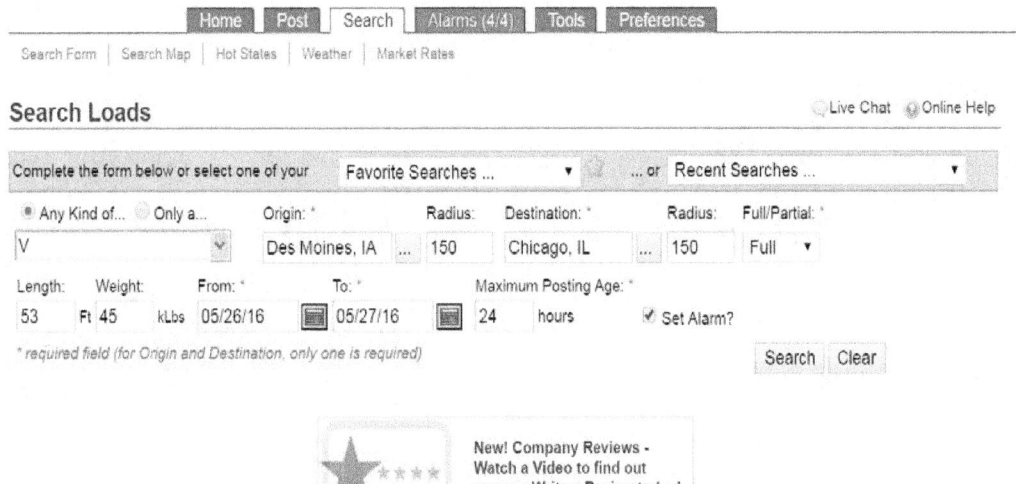

DAT TruckersEdge®

Home | Post | Search | Alarms | Tools | Preferences

Hot States | Weather | Market Rates | CarrierWatch

Post A Truck

Live Chat | Online Help

Available: *	Truck Type: *	Origin: *	Destination:	Full/Partial: *	Length: *	Weight: *	# Trucks:
05/26/16	Van: V	Souix Falls, IA	Detroit, MI	Full	53 Ft	50 kLbs	1

Alarm Details:
- Off
- On, radius of 100 mi

Cube: ft3

Preferred Contact Method: 444-555-6666

Comments: Ext. 4707

Reference #:

Post For: 1 day(s)

* required field

[Post] [Clear]

Results 5/26/2016 at 2:29 PM

View Result Details | Printable Version

Your search returned 20 standard matches plus 561 expanded matches. Displaying 1 through 100 of 581.

< Previous Page | Next Page >

Age (h:mm)	P/U Date	Truck Type	F/P	DH (O)	Origin	Trip	Destination	DH (D)	Contact	Credit Score	DTP	Ft	kLbs	Company	TIA	PC	Factor	Mkt Rates
0:06	05/27	V	F	0	Des Moines, IA	343	Chicago, IL	0	(877) 896-1632	103	32	45	40	Fetch Logistics Inc	TIA		✓	R
0:31	05/27	V	F	0	Des Moines, IA	343	Chicago, IL	0	(877) 896-1632	103	32	45	40	Fetch Logistics Inc	TIA		✓	R
1:29	05/27	V	F	0	Des Moines, IA	367	Valparaiso, IN	49	(877) 896-1632	103	32	53	45	Fetch Logistics Inc	TIA		✓	R
2:46	05/27	V	F	0	Des Moines, IA	375	Cudahy, WI	92	(206) 535-8115	96	37	53	30	SCR AIR SERVICES INC	TIA		✓	R
1:21	05/27	V	F	35	Ames, IA	530	Bluffton, IN	191	(888) 647-8782	100	31	53	42	Matson Integrated ...	TIA			R
1:21	05/27	V	F	35	Ames, IA	530	Bluffton, IN	191	(888) 647-8782	100	31	53	42	Matson Integrated ...	TIA		✓	R
0:16	05/26	VR	F	83	Hedrick, IA	218	Normal, IL	131	(800) 836-9612	103	29	48	45	PIONEER TRANSFER	TIA	✓		R
2:20	05/27	VR	F	83	Hedrick, IA	218	Normal, IL	131	(800) 228-2761	100	24	48	40	Mannings Truck Bro...				R
0:15	05/27	V	F	90	Ottumwa, IA	329	Valparaiso, IN	49	(719) 766-8404	103	29		42	UTI TRANSPORT SOLUTIONS	TIA		✓	R
0:16	05/27	V	F	90	Ottumwa, IA	329	Valparaiso, IN	49	(904) 435-9548	99	33	53	42	PLS Logistics Services	TIA		✓	R
1:51	05/26	V	F	125	Cedar Falls, IA	448	Wabash, IN	156	(855) 894-3658	100	33		44	BNSF LOGISTICS			✓	R
1:40	05/26	V	F	131	Cedar Rapids, IA	227	Lincoln, IL	168	(800) 518-4287	100	32	53	40	Circle 8 Logistics Inc			✓	R
0:06	05/27	V	F	136	Mt Pleasant, IA	320	Brown Deer, WI	104	(877) 279-8144	100	27	53	44	ABF Multimodal Inc	TIA			R
0:04	05/27	VR	F	137	Algona, IA	409	Normal, IL	131	(800) 836-9612	103	29	48	45	PIONEER TRANSFER	TIA	✓		R
0:55	05/27	V	F	154	Muscatine, IA	310	Lebanon, IN	153	(800) 311-2128	103	32	53		CH Robinson Company	TIA	✓		R
0:15	05/27	V	F	167	Burlington, IA	237	Burnham, IL	20	(719) 766-8404	103	29		42	UTI TRANSPORT SOLUTIONS	TIA		✓	R
0:16	05/27	V	F	167	Burlington, IA	240	Chicago, IL	0	(904) 435-9548	99	33	53	42	PLS Logistics Services	TIA		✓	R
0:26	05/27	V	F	167	Burlington, IA	200	Montgomery, IL	45	(866) 603-2095	91	65	53		JB Hunt Transport ...			✓	R
0:30	05/27	V	F	187	W Union, IA	458	Bluffton, IN	191	(888) 220-4640	98	38	53	8	Ultra Logistics Inc			✓	R
0:04	05/27	V	F	204	Canton, MO	309	Elmhurst, IL	20	(616) 940-1200	103	32	53		CH Robinson Company	TIA		✓	R

TruckingSuccess.com

7054 North 28th Drive

Phoenix, AZ 85051

Tel. (602) 864-8056

support@truckingsuccess.com

Information presented in this seminar is current at the time of printing. Specifications subject to change. The Dispatch Seminar is part of The Dispatch Manual TXu1-335-556 Copyright 2020 TruckingSuccess.com All Rights Reserved

TruckingSuccess.com

Dispatch Manual
2020 Edition

A Business Management Manual For The Independent Owner Operator

Dispatch Manual©

2020 Edition
A Comprehensive Resource And Instructions Manual for Independent Owner-Operators

TruckingSuccess.com

Copyright © 2020 – TruckingSuccess.com – All rights reserved. Reproduction in any manner, in whole or in part, without permission is prohibited.

Table of Contents

Introduction

Chapter 1 – Transportation Industry Overview

Chapter 2 – Tools Of The Trade

Chapter 3 – Professionalism

Chapter 4 – Load Availability

Chapter 5 – Finding the Right Loads

Chapter 6 – Booking Loads

Chapter 7 – Freight Handling

Chapter 8 – Freight Delivery

Dear Business Partner:

Congratulations on making the decision to learn more about an important aspect of your trucking business with the goal to maximize your profitability. Also allow me to express our heartfelt gratitude to you for purchasing our Dispatch Manual. We are confident that the knowledge and insights about the transportation industry gained from studying this publication will allow you to work smarter, not harder to succeed as an Owner Operator. It will empower you to make the right choices for your business and give you the confidence to apply this information in your day-to-day operations.

This business publication provides all the tools and information an independent Owner Operator needs to successfully dispatch his or her own truck(s). It explains how to set up your mobile office, lists important business contacts, and provides information about laws and regulations as well as required documents. It describes how to provide excellent customer service, build successful business relationships and effectively manage time and stress. It explains freight volume and facts affecting load availability. It guides you through the process of obtaining your own loads and dispatching your own truck(s). And you also learn about proper freight handling and important delivery procedures. Finally, this publication dispels myths and common misconceptions about the trucking industry, provides you with facts to disprove "truck stop" gossip, and makes the process of dispatching transparent.

Thank you again for choosing our publication "The Dispatch Manual," and best wishes for your success,

The Staff of TruckingSuccess.com

Chapter 1 – Transportation Industry Overview

Professional Organizations

Every industry, trade, profession, and occupation has established business practices and ethical standards that set certain guidelines how business should be conducted. The primary purpose of these practices and standards is to establish trust among the industry to promote good business relationships and facilitate business transactions. The Transport Intermediaries Association (TIA) is the professional and educational organization of the $80.6 billion third party logistics industry, representing transport intermediaries. Among other activities, this organization provides education, research, and services to help its members succeed. The members of TIA include domestic freight forwarders, motor carriers, perishable commodity brokers, logistics management companies, as well as other transportation-related businesses.

The TIA publishes an annual membership directory, which includes freight brokers. As a condition of membership, all TIA members are required to sign and adhere to the TIA Code of Ethics. The Ethics Committee of TIA arbitrates disputes and ensures that members adhere to the Code of Ethics. The articles of the Code of Ethics have been adopted by the TIA to promote and maintain high standards of professional service and ethical business conduct among its members and can be found in the Membership Directory (source: TIA Membership Directory 2014).

Industry Image

Programs such as Trucker Buddy International and Goodyear Highway Hero seek to promote a positive image of the trucking industry among the general public. Nevertheless, widely accepted myths and stereotypes about the trucking industry in general and professional drivers in particular are shaped by popular culture, particularly movies and television series. While some of the stereotypes are positive and portray the trucker as an upstanding and even heroic member of the community, others are negative, such as the portrayal of a tanker truck driver in the motion picture *Thelma and Louise*. Although this is a fictional character, the negative portrayal may contribute to the belief that all drivers behave that way. Unfortunately, the negative perceptions seem to prevail in the general public and the news media perpetrate these stereotypes when reporters unfamiliar with the trucking industry write sensational stories about events involving big rigs without checking the facts. Even industry publications contribute to the misinformation in the industry when they public articles with unsubstantiated information and without providing supporting documentation and facts. Although documentaries such as *Wheels of Change* documenting the how trucking shaped America and *A Mistress Called the Road* portraying the hardships of life on the road are on the market, they fail to reach mass audiences.

Truckers spend a lot of time alone on the road, so they like to socialize when they get to a truck stop or have to wait at a loading dock. Naturally, they talk about their trucks, loads they are pulling, and how much money they are making. Of course, there is nothing wrong with socializing – it is only human to share information. And while you may learn something new once in a while, many times you will hear half-truths or lies that may make you feel bad about your own situation. Only when you know the facts about the trucking industry, will you be able to distinguish the professional drivers from the nonsense talkers. Walk away as soon as you can when you encounter nonsense talkers and do not waste your time to listen to their gossip because you cannot learn anything new from these individuals. You have heard the old adage "time is money" many times, and you have better things to do than trying to educate them.

Dispatch History

Over the past fifteen years, tremendous changes occurred in the way loads are dispatched and how Owner-Operators obtain loads. In the "old" days before the telecommunications and Internet revolution, Owner-Operators usually worked with one or two brokers located in their hometown to obtain loads. After unloading, the trucker went to a nearby truck stop to call his broker for the next load. Some truckers had pagers, but cellular phone were not yet available. Some Owner-Operators also obtained loads from computer load boards found at almost every truck stop throughout the United States. The larger freight brokerage companies posted their loads via a computer network on these load boards and the bigger truck stops had rows of telephone booths so truckers could make their phone calls. Additionally, Owner-Operators called their brokers from the road using pay phones to get load updates or other delivery instructions. When facsimile machines became available at the truck stops in the 1980's, Owner-Operators were able to receive documents on the road. In those days, instant credit checks were not available and truckers relied on expensive publications listing the credit ratings of brokers and carriers. Overall, the pace was slower but more inconvenient.

Owner-Operator Income

Recently, a professional magazine did a cover story about apparently very successful leased- on Owner Operators. One of the truckers featured on the cover of the magazine and profiled in the story told the reporter he expects to gross $350,000.00 in 2014 with a net income of $115,000.00 while he is leased on to a trucking company. To industry insiders, this sounds incredible, but consider the source. The magazine publisher is a trucking company. So, how much money do Owner Operators really earn?

According to published statistics, Owner Operator net income per month from the third quarter of 2013 to the second quarter of 2013 ranged between $4,000.00 and $4,250.00, with a net income per mile between 37 cents to 44 cents. Another Owner Operator profiled in the above- mentioned article expected his take home pay to be $48,000.00 net for 2014, and this figure is realistic. Based on our experience, an independent Owner Operator doing his or her dispatching following our dispatch methods can gross between $180,000.00 to $230,000.00 a year. It is difficult to estimate the annual net income based on the above-mentioned gross income, because operating costs can vary widely. Obviously, an Owner Operator who runs on paid equipment has lower operating costs and costs per mile than a trucker who runs financed equipment. Nevertheless, an Owner Operator averaging 12,000 loaded and empty miles a month should gross $20,000.00 to $22,000.00 a month. These figures are significantly better than published statistics, which show average gross revenue of $10,500.00 to $12,500.00 a month between the third quarter of 2013 and the second quarter of 2013. These income levels are also different when pulling a dry van or a reefer. A dry van will average $1.50 per mile, a reefer should average $1.85 to $2.20 per mile. Always calculate a round trip divided by all miles.

Chapter 2 – Tools Of the Trade - Your Mobile Office

In order to effectively dispatch your truck(s) from the road, you will need the proper tools and space in your truck where you can set up your mobile office. The main components of your office equipments will be a good and sturdy laptop computer with a wireless connection to the Internet, a reliable printer, as well as a quality cellular phone with a good rate plan. For your convenience, you may also invest in a wireless facsimile machine so you can send and receive faxes from brokers and shippers. If a fax machine is not in your budget, you can buy a fax software system that works with your e-mail system, or you can sign up with one of the Internet fax services such as myfax.com and receive faxes via your e-mail account and print them out.

Additionally, you will need to set up your business e-mail account, choosing an e-mail address that is professional and reflects your business name. We recommend you also set up a private e-mail account to keep your personal correspondence separate from your business. Also, your voice mail message on your business cell phone should be recorded in a professional manner.

You will also need to designate an area in your truck cabin as your working space and set up a document storage and filing system to keep your paperwork organized. Then you will need the basic office materials such as printer paper, pens, notepapers, paper clips, stapler, hole puncher, and clipboards. Even if you use one of the various routing software programs available for the transportation industry, you should always have a current Rand McNally's Motor Carriers' Road Atlas in your truck.

Important Business Contacts

A variety of organizations, businesses, and governmental agencies provide services, information, products that are vital to the independent Owner Operator and dispatcher. Government agencies such as the Federal Highway Administration promulgate laws, and trucking-related organizations such as the Owner Operator Independent Driver Association (OOID) lobby on behalf of their members and disseminate information via their publication and web sites.

Below is a list of these important business contacts by categories.

Government Agencies

The Federal Motor Carrier Safety Administration (FMCSA) provides background information including license, bond, and insurance information about brokers and motor carriers free of cost.

Federal Motor Carrier
Safety Administration
Washington, D.C.
Phone: (202) 366-9805 (applications)
(202) 385-2423 (insurance) Online: www.li-public.fmcas.dot.gov

The U.S. Department of Agriculture (USDA) also provides on line background checks, including licensing and recent disciplinary actions against brokers free of cost.

U.S. Department of Agriculture Fruits and Vegetables

Washington, DC
Phone: (202) 720-6873
Online: www.ams.usda.gov/fv/paca.htm

The USDA also provides freight rate recommendations on line at http://www.ams.usda.gov/mnreports/wa_fv190.txt

Associations/Organizations

The Owner-Operator Independent Drivers Association publishes a bimonthly/monthly magazine called *Land Line* in addition to providing trucking business consulting, on line background checks, assistance with collections of unpaid freight bills, and attorney referrals. The annual membership fee is $45.00.

Owner-Operator Independent Drivers Association (OOIDA)
P.O. Box 1000 - Grain Valley, MO 64029-9900
Phone: (800) 440-5791

The Transportation Intermediaries Association (TIA) is the professional and educational organization of the third party logistics industry, representing transport intermediaries. Among other activities, this organization provides education, research and services to help its members succeed.

The TIA publishes an annual membership directory, which includes a listing of brokers. The directory is on line at www.tianet.org.

Transportation Intermediaries Association
1625 Prince Street, Suite 200
Alexandria, VA 22314-2818
Phone: (703) 299-5700
Fax: (703) 836-0123

The Goodyear Highway Hero Program honors truck drivers who keep the nation's economy moving with daily commerce and who come to the rescue of fellow motorists. Nomination forms and program details may be obtained by calling the Goodyear Highway Hero Hot Line at (330) 796-8183. The nomination form also is available on the program's web site at www.goodyear.com/ truck/whatsnew/heroes.html.

Services

TruckingSuccess.com provides a variety of services, products and information for the Owner-Operator and the transportation industry. For more information, log on to www.truckingsuccess.com.

RTS Credit Service provides on line background checks on freight brokers using a rating system about each broker's payment habits. RTS charges an annual fee of $299.00 or $35.00 a month for this service. To subscribe, call (888) 492-7006 or go online to www.rtscredit.com.

RBCS Transportation Brokers Rating Service provides business ethics and payment practices on over 4,600 transportation brokers with the RBCS Transportation Brokers Rating Service. RBCS publishes the *Redbook* directory twice a year and also provides broker ratings on line with full access to their website 24/7. For more information, call 1 (800) 252-1925 or go on-line to www.rbcs.com or www.redbooktrucking.com.

FMCSA provides on line background checks, including license, bond and insurance information (see previous section for contact information).

USDA provides on-line background checks, including licensing and recent disciplinary actions, as well as freight rate recommendations (see previous section for contact information).

OOIDA provides a variety of services for the independent Owner-Operator. Please visit OOIDA on-line at www.ooida.com for more details.

RTS Factoring Service offers financial services, which can improve your cash flow and simplify your billing process. To learn more about factoring your Accounts Receivables and to sign up for RTS Factoring Service, please go on-line to www.rtscredit.com .

www.truckersedge.net/promo123 offers a thirty-day free trial of its Internet load board. $34.95 a month after and you may cancel anytime.
Go to: www.truckersedge.net/promo123

Truckstop.com provides trucking business consulting and on-line background checks. The on-line credit check service costs $35.00 a month. For more information call 1 (800) 203-2540 or go on-line to www.truckstop.com.

PostEverywhere.com provides a service, which allows you to post your truck on about twenty-five different on-line load boards. To learn more about this service and to sign up, please go to www.PostEverywhere.com.

Products

TruckingSuccess.com publishes a variety of business manuals and products for independent Owner- Operator trucking operations. To view the product line, please go to: www.truckingsuccess.com.

Wheels of Change video documents how trucking shaped America following the epic adventure of trucks and truckers as they carve their way through a country of unpaved roads, carry the fight in WWII, and haul America into the 21st century. Available at: www.truckingsuccess.com.

A Mistress Called The Road compact disc is a documentary of the life on the road and provides a positive look a the trucking life exploring the powerful pull of the road and subtly reveals its emotional draw in a way only someone who has lived the life could. Available at: www.truckingsuccess.com.

J.J. Keller & Associates, Inc. publishes and sells a variety of trucking-related forms, education materials and business products. For a list of products, please go online to www.truckingsuccess.com and click on the **J.J. Keller icon**.

A variety of companies provide useful services at competitive rates and many offer a thirty- day trial period. TruckingSuccess.com recommends you choose the service that provides you with accurate, timely, and reliable information at a reasonable price.

Professional Publications

TruckingSuccess.com publishes business manuals for the independent Owner-Operator. For more information, please go on-line to www.truckingsuccess.com.

Land Line magazine published by OOIDA (see above for contact information) *Heavy Duty Trucking* magazine – the business magazine of trucking – send subscription inquires or orders to Heavy Duty Trucking, P.O. 16899, North Hollywood, CA 91615, phone (818) 760-0472, online: www.truckinginfo.com

FleetOwner publication provides daily trucking news – to subscribe either to the publication or the newsletter, go to www.FLEETOWNER.COM.

Overdrive magazine published by Randall & Reilly – for subscription inquiries and information call (800) 517-4979 or go on-line to www.overdrive.com.

The Trucker is a semi-monthly national newspaper for the truckload freight industry published by Trucker Publications, Inc., at 1123 S. University, Suite 320, Little Rock, AR 72204- 1610. To subscribe, please call (800) 666-2770 or go on-line: www.thetrucker.com.

Laws and Regulations

Broker Registration and Bond: The law requires the Secretary of Transportation to register transportation brokers only if they provide proof of a bond or some other form of approved security. The current broker bond of $75,000.00 was set in 2013.

There are now more than 15,000 brokers and the $75,000.00 bond comes nowhere close to covering the amount of unpaid liabilities incurred by many brokers today; therefore, thorough broker background checks are an important business tool for the Owner-Operator to avoid nonpayment. It is also important to know that the Federal Motor Carrier Safety Administration does not actively pursue delinquent brokers and brokers who default on their liabilities often do not suffer any consequences and continue their illegal behavior, setting up a new brokerage operation in a different location with a new name.

Broker Contracts: Depending on the clauses of a freight-hauling contract, shippers can be forced to pay twice for the transportation service if a broker does not pay the motor carrier, under Title 49 of the U.S Code. The Transportation Intermediaries Association proposed a new model broker-carrier contract with clauses in the contract such as: "Carrier shall not seek payment from shipper if shipper can prove payment to broker." Owner-Operators signing such contracts waive their rights and remedies under Title 49 of the U.S. Code; therefore, they should carefully read the entire contract to ensure it does not contain clauses detrimental to the Owner-Operators legal rights.

Broker Paperwork: Federal law requires brokers to maintain certain paperwork relating to transportation services brokered and make the paperwork available to the parties involved. According to 49 CFR 371.3, the information requested includes:

- The name, address and registration number of the consigner;
- The bill of lading or freight bill number;
- The amount of compensation received by the broker for the service performed and the name of the payer;
- The amount of compensation for any non-brokerage services and the name of the payer; and
- The amount of freight charges collected and the date collected.

Required Documents

Vendor Set-up Package: The process of booking a load includes completing a set of legal documents and contracts. When you deal with a brokerage firm for the first time, you have to complete a Vendor Set-up Package as well as provide information about your business. Your own package of credentials includes a copy of your Carrier Authority issued by the USDOT/FMCSA, a certificate of liability insurance, a completed W-9 form, and several references.

The Vendor Set-up package includes a data sheet that you must complete, the broker/motor carrier agreement (you must place your initials on every page), the brokerage firm's credentials such as a copies of their Broker's License issued by the Federal Highway Administration, surety bond certificate, certificate of liability insurance, a blank W-9 form, and credit references.

Insurance Certificate: The brokerage firm requires that your insurance company include their firm in your insurance certificate as a Certificate Holder. We advise that you call your insurance company and have them fax the insurance certificate with the name of he Certificate Holder (the brokerage firm) directly to the broker.

Chapter 3 – Professionalism

When you act as your own dispatcher, you will have daily contacts with brokers, agents, insurance company representatives, and shippers. The characteristics that make you a successful Owner-Operator will also contribute to your success in the dispatch business. Excellent customer service skills will help you build good business relationships and establish a good reputation for your business. Effective written communication skills will ensure that your business transactions are processed efficiently and correctly. Furthermore, managing your time effectively to incorporate your dispatch activities into your daily schedule will increase your productivity and pofitability.

Customer Service Skills

Almost all of the dispatch activities are conducted over the telephone and via fax machine. Most likely you will never have face-to-face meetings with your business contacts; therefore, it is important that you communicate in a professional manner to make a good first impression. Your verbal communications should be polite and courteous regardless how the other person treats you. Your written communications should be neat and legible, using proper business language and grammar. Avoid coarse and foul language even if you do not get treated right. You should be assertive but not aggressive. If you cannot resolve a conflict in a professional manner, consider not doing business with a company that does not treat you with respect, rather than getting into verbal arguments over the telephone.

Building Business Relationships

Good verbal and written communications skills will help you establish productive business relationships and ensure your business transactions are handled properly. All business relationships are built on mutual trust and the understanding that the parties involved live up to their respective responsibilities. As such, you should conduct your business dealings with integrity and fairness, following through and honoring all of your business agreements. Again, if you have a bad experience with a company whodoes not follow generally accepted business practices; it is better not to do business with them. However, keep in mind that at times when you call a brokerage company about a specific problem, you may speak with an individual who is poorly trained and does not have the necessary expertise to assist you. In this case, do not waste valuable time explaining your situation because this individual will not be able to resolve the particular issue. In our experience, this happens often during weekends and after regular business hours. Most large brokerage companies maintain twenty-four-hour service, but the agents available after regular business hours are not as experienced and familiar with the specifics of your load as your broker/ agent. Rather than wasting your time and getting frustrated with an agent who is unable to help you, we suggest you wait and call your broker/agent the next morning to resolve the issue properly.

In the competitive transportation industry, maintaining friendly business relationships with brokers may make a difference during times when loads are scarce or rates are down. We recommend you create a telephone contact list of all the companies and brokers with whom you have established positive business relationships. You will find that over time this list will be a very valuable business asset.

When you negotiate financial details such as freight rates, detention pay, fuel surcharges, payment for additional stops, and mileage pay for dead-heading, you should always keep the "bigger picture" in mind to avoid getting "hung up" on minor financial details. Often inexperienced Owner-Operators lose good loads or valuable time over minor financial differences. For example, the standard rate for overnight detention time is $250.00. Although an Owner-Operator may feel that (s)he should receive a higher pay for their valuable time and ask for $400.00 or $500.00, it is useless to argue this point with the shipper or broker, because they will not pay more than the current standard rate. It makes more business sense to accept this reality and move on to the next load. Remember, you only produce revenue when the wheels of your truck are turning.

Providing excellent customer service also helps to establish and maintain good business relationships. Owner-Operators who provide good service develop a good reputation over time and generate good will. The basic elements of service include picking up and delivering loads on time, following delivery instructions, making required check-in calls, and communicating any unforeseen delays to the other party.

Time Management

Finding the right load(s) takes time, experience, and some planning. When you dispatch your own truck from the road, you will have to fit your dispatch activities into your daily driving routine; however, eventually you will work out a system that will fit your travel schedules. To complicate matters more, you have to take into consideration time zones, regular business hours, as well as your delivery schedules.

We recommend that you schedule a one-hour stop about every two days during the morning hours to review on-line load boards and make phone calls. You should call brokerage companies between 9:00 AM and 11:00 AM their local time because everybody is in the office during the morning hours taking care of business. In our experience, most load-booking business is done before lunch breaks. After lunch, you may place courtesy calls to brokers/agents to advise them that your truck is available so they may call you when loads become available later in the day or the next morning. To avoid costly layovers and waiting time at the loading dock, you must book your loads in advance, not on the day you unload at your destination. This means you should start searching for a new load three days prior to unloading your current load. If you cannot find a good-paying load on the first day, you still have two days left to research load boards and call brokers.

Stress Management

Life on the road is already stressful without the added dispatch duties.
What can you do to make it all work? There are several steps you can take to reduce stress and accomplish your daily tasks successfully. Planning ahead and establishing a daily schedule and adhering to it will help you stay on track. Utilize the organizational system you devised when you set up your mobile office and prioritize tasks to effectively manage your time. Having a place for everything and putting it back where it belongs when you no longer use it will save you time every day. As you gain more experience with your dispatching duties, it will become part of your daily routine. In summary, experience, planning ahead and adhering to a daily schedule as well as maintaining an organizational system will help you avoid stressful situations. What may your daily schedule look like when you are on the West Coast? You unloaded at 4:00 AM and are headed to a truck stop where you arrive at 5:00 AM. You freshen up and eat breakfast. From approximately 6:00 AM to :00 AM., you scan on-line load boards and make phone calls to shippers and brokers to secure a load when you arrive at your next location. Following the Hours of Service regulations, you sleep ten hours. Then you drive to pick up your next load at 6:00 PM.

Chapter 4 – Load Availability

How many times have you wondered why you sit empty at a truck stop for several days before your broker finds another load for you and why you do not get the high-paying loads other truckers boast about hauling all the time? You may have guessed it -- there are no simple answers to your questions! Only when you gain insight into how the transportation industry works will you understand how the business principle of supply and demand affects how much a load pays and how many loads are available at any given time.

Freight Volume - Cyclicality: Although there are tens of thousands of loads available at any given day, economic cycles and seasonal demand determine the volume of available freight. When the economy expands rapidly, freight volume increases and lots of loads are available at very good rates because shippers compete for tight truckload capacity. On the contrary, when the economy slows down and contracts, freight volume decreases and rates go down. The American Trucking Association tracks for-hire truck tonnage and issues a quarterly Truck Tonnage Index for the trucking industry.

Economic Activity: Some economic activities generate more freight volume than others.
Construction, manufacturing and even international trade depend on trucking to transport raw materials, manufactured goods, and merchandise. In fact, trucks move about seventy percent of all domestic freight, including wholesale and retail goods. Strong consumer spending on high-ticket items, food, clothing and other goods has a positive effect on freight volume. When interest rates and gas prices are high, consumer spending drops, resulting in a weaker freight volume but increased transportation capacity and lower freight rates.

Seasonal Demand in addition to cyclical changes in freight levels, seasonal demand affects the freight volume and rates. Every year, during the peak growing season in California, thousands of Owner-Operators head toward the West Coast for the high- paying produce loads to the East Coast. Word about $6,000.00 produce loads to the East Coast spreads like wildfire and soon there is a glut of trucks on the West Coast. What is the result? Rates drop immediately due to excessive truck capacity. Shippers now can choose between numerous carriers who accept almost any rate just to get out of California. As a result, loads that paid $6,000.00 one week, go for $4,000.00 to $5,000.00 the next week.

Generally, demand for freight capacity changes with the seasons. From January to April, demand is slow. It picks up when the produce season starts on the West Coast and peaks during the early summer. Freight volume slows down again after the Fourth of July, picks up again in the fall and remains strong during the pre-holiday months and through the Christmas rush.

Freight Volume by States: Additionally, location affects the volume of available freight. The Top 15 Activity States based on incoming and outgoing loads posts are Texas, Ohio, Illinois, Pennsylvania, California, Georgia, Indiana, Florida, North Carolina, Tennessee, New York, Maryland, Missouri, Michigan, Wisconsin, and Arkansas. However, some states such as Texas, Pennsylvania, Georgia, Florida, and North Carolina have more incoming than outgoing loads. That means if you deliver a load into these states, you will have a difficult time finding a suitable outgoing load. On the other hand, some states such as Ohio, Illinois, New York, Wisconsin, Arkansas, and Indiana have more outgoing than incoming loads. That means if you deliver a load into these states you will easily find a good outgoing load in these states. States such as California, Tennessee, Missouri, and Michigan have a relatively balanced ratio of incoming and outgoing loads. The Top 15 Activity States Index is published in the *Heavy Duty Trucking* magazine.

Equipment

In addition to the above-mentioned factors, the type of equipment an Owner-Operator owns and operates narrows or widens the pool of freight that is available at any given day, and it determines how much revenue (s)he generates throughout the business year. Most Owner-Operators choose what type of equipment they prefer to operate at the beginning of their career and specialize in either flatbed, step deck, tanker truck, dry van or refrigerated van transportation. Each equipment type has its own drawbacks as well as advantages. The rates for flatbed and step deck freight are very good; however, it is often difficult to find connecting loads without having to "deadhead" hundreds of miles. Step deck freight also often requires special tarps and expensive safety equipment.

Independent Owner-Operators generally do not operate tanker trucks for obvious reasons
– the type of freight they can haul is too restricted. Although dry vans have been very popular, it is difficult to make a living hauling dry freight because the rate is often less than $1.00 a mile, which is below the cost-per-mile for many Owner-Operators. The fifty-three-foot refrigerated van or "reefer" is the most versatile equipment for the independent Owner-Operator. It can handle dry, refrigerated, and frozen freight, making it easier to find suitable loads anywhere and anytime. However, it takes skill and experience to handle perishable cargo properly so it does not sustain damage in transit.

Owner-Operator Specifics

Finally, the Owner-Operator's personal preferences as well as business parameters determine how many loads (s)he can select from the large pool of available freight. Personal preferences include weather conditions, length of time away from home, and family obligations. Less experienced drivers may prefer to stay on the southern routes during the winter months rather than going to the Midwest and Northeast where there is a change of running into snow and ice. Family obligations are also a consideration and determine how long an Owner-Operator is willing to stay out on the road and away from home. Business considerations such as permits, cost per mile, Hours of Service, and a shipper's credit worthiness affect load selection and trip planning. An Owner-Operator who has permits for all forty-eight states will have a wider selection of freight than an Owner-Operator who only runs in the eleven Western States. Cost-permile calculations will eliminate many of the loads offered because it is not profitable to haul cheap loads and a shipper's credit rating will further narrow the pool of available loads.

Hours of Service Regulations

Furthermore, delivery time frames of loads that are deemed suitable have to fit into the Owner-Operator's Hours of Service schedule. This requires a calculation of distance and daily miles to delivery time frames. When an Owner-Operator has been on duty for almost sixty hours in seven consecutive days or seventy hours in eight consecutive days, it will not make any sense to book a cross-country load with a tight delivery schedule. In this case, the Owner-Operator should post the truck and inform his or her contacts that (s)he is available to take the next load after having been thirty-four or more consecutive hours off-duty.

Chapter 5 – Finding the Right Loads

Freight Rates

The state of the economy, seasonal demand, physical location, and transportation capacity affect freight rates at any given day. Generally, rates for cross-country loads from the West to the East Coast are $1.85 to $2.20 per mile or $5,550 to $6,600.00 for the entire trip. However, rates for loads originating on the East Coast and going to the West Coast are thirty to forty percent lower than loads originating on the West Coast and going to the East Coast. Generally, rates for cross- country loads from the East to the West Coast are $1.25 to $1.65 per mile or $3,750.00 to $4,950.00 for the entire trip. In some states such as Florida or Texas rates for outgoing loads are $1.30 or less because of excessive transportation capacity in these locations. Many Owner-Operators are not aware of a state's incoming/outgoing rate differential and accept these cheap long-haul loads just to get out of these states. They haul these loads without making any profit because the cost per mile for most Owner-Operators is now $1.20 and they may even lose some of the profit from the better- paying load they brought into the state. Only the shippers will benefit and the Owner-Operator may barely break even.

Positioning

Often an Owner-Operator may locate a good-paying load to a suitable destination, but (s)he is several hundred miles away from the pickup location. This poses a challenge but there are several options for handling this situation. One option is to continue researching the load boards and perhaps locate another load with a nearby pickup location.

However, additional research may not yield another suitable load and the original load is the best offer available at the time. In this case you may chose the second option, which involves dead-heading to the pickup destination, but driving empty and without pay is not the most economical solution considering today's high fuel prices. The third and more practical option involves finding a short-haul load to the area where the good-paying load is located. In this scenario, the Owner-Operator may intentionally book one of these cheap loads for a short haul only to position the truck in a location where (s)he can pick up a better-paying load.

Round-trip Concept

Considering all these factors, how do you find loads that pay well and increase your revenue? First you have to change your approach and adopt a new strategy. Instead of using a load-by-load approach, you should adopt the **round-trip concept** to determine if load rates meet your criteria. The round trip calculation only works when you dispatch your own truck because it requires planning ahead. To do it right, you take a load cross-country from the West to the East Coast and you split the return trip into two or three sections.

Below is an example of dispatching using the round-trip concepts to enhance your revenue.

1. Start in California with a load to Massachusetts
   Approx. 3,000 miles at $2.00 per mile

   $6,000.00

1. Next take a load from Massachusetts to Ohio
   Approx. 400 miles at $1.20 per mile

   $480.00

1. Next take a load from Ohio to Colorado
   Approx. 1,400 miles at $1.60 per mile

   $2,240.00

1. Complete round-trip with a load from Colorado to California
   Approx. 1,200.00 at $1.35 per mile

   $1,620.00

Total revenue for cross-country roundtrip   **$10,340.0**

Comparison Trip

1	Start in California with a load to Massachusetts Approx. 3,000 miles at $2.00 per mile	$6,000.00
2	Backhaul load to California Approx. 3,000 miles at $1.10 per mile	$3,300.00

Total revenue for cross-country roundtrip $9,300.00

Difference $1,040.00

The Owner-Operator who took the straight back-haul to California earned $1,040.00 less on one round-trip. If he makes two round-trips a month, he will lose $2,080.00 of revenue per month, or $24,960.00 of revenue in one year. Even if you haul freight only in certain regions of the United States, always calculate the round-trip revenue to determine if a load is acceptable. You will be more flexible in your decision-making using this approach and it may avoid argument about freight rates with brokers and shippers.

Load Resources

Load Boards: Modern communications technology has simplified access to load information. Independent Owner-Operators only need a computer (laptop) and (wireless)

Internet to view thousands of load listings on on-line load boards every day. Among the dozens of on-line load boards, getloaded.com and truckstop.com are the more popular services among Owner-Operators. These load board companies charge a fee of approximately $30.00 per month and may offer a thirty-day trial period at no cost. The load boards also provide credit ratings, but they are not always accurate.

Post Your Own Truck: When you sign up with an on-line load board, you can also post your own truck days in advance of your next delivery destination so brokers and shippers can call you about loads they have available when you arrive at your destination. You will get calls with freight offers and you may even receive a good-paying load without much effort of your own, saving you valuable time researching suitable loads.

You may also utilize services such as PostEverywhere.com, which automatically submits your truck information to approximately twenty-five on-line load boards. When you use these services, you should always post your truck after you get loaded so the information is available on-line two to three days before you deliver the current load and your truck is empty again. This allows you to plan ahead and make use of the round-trip dispatch system.

Brokers and Logistics Companies: In addition to the on-line load resources, honest brokers and third-party logistics companies continue to be valuable contacts for obtaining loads. Most of the larger brokerage and logistics companies offer various payment options including quick pay, which may be to the Owner-Operator's advantage. The Transportation Intermediaries Association (TIA) publishes an annual membership directory, which lists hundreds of brokers who have undergone background checks and adhere to the TIA's Code of Ethics. Large brokerage firms and logistics companies generate loads through their national and international contacts. Their offices usually operate twenty-four hours a day, seven days a week. When you establish business relationships, start creating your own contact and reference list of companies that you found reliable and credit worthy so you can use their services again without doing additional credit checks.

Shipper-Direct Loads: Many carriers would like to get loads directly from shippers and eliminate the middleman who takes a cut from the freight rate. While it is not impossible for independent Owner-Operators to work directly with shippers, it is a difficult undertaking because most shippers prefer to work with larger carriers. One reason is that the shippers are able to negotiate better rates with the carrier for large freight volume, and the carrier guarantees that the shipper's loads get picked up and delivered. Even when an Owner-Operator finds shipper-direct loads, they are only one-way and (s)he still has to use a broker for the back-haul load. However, the financial aspects of shipper-direct loads will break the deal for most Owner-Operators. Shippers generally pay in sixty to ninety days! In the capital-intensive transportation industry where thousands of dollars are at stake with every load, sixty to ninety days is too long to wait for payment for most Owner-Operators. Should the shipper experience financial difficulties and be unable to pay, the Owner-Operator faces financial ruin.

Researching Loads

Perusing on-line load boards is the first step in researching loads to determine what freight is available to tentative destinations. Make sure you ignore all listings without credit ratings as well as credit ratings below 90. A credit listing of "N/A" indicates the company listing the load is new and has not established a credit history. Entering into a business relationship with such companies is a high risk because they have no payment history to ensure you get paid. And if you factor your freight bills, the factoring company will not accept your paperwork. Companies with credit ratings between 85 and 100 are considered low risk because they have established a financial track record of paying their freight bills. Companies with credit ratings below 85 present a moderate to high financial risk and Owner-Operators doing business with these companies may have difficulty collecting their freight bills.

The next step is making phone calls to get more details from the broker or agent about potential loads you selected from on-line load boards. While the broker gives you the load information over the phone, you must make your assessment based on the factors discussed in the previous chapters to determine if it is a "good" load. The load information includes details about the number of pickups and drops; pickup location, date and time; delivery location, date and time; the type of product, total weight, freight rate, as well as other shipping instructions, and the shipper's Motor Carrier identification number. Be aware that you only have a few seconds to decide if you want to haul a particular load. If you cannot make up your mind right away and you call back later, the load will no longer be available because you are one of many Owner-Operator inquiring about the same loads.

In case you do not find suitable loads on-line, you must start calling brokerage and logistics firms to determine what freight is available to your tentative destination. If you have already established your own contact list, first call your own contacts and check what loads they have available. And, if you posted your truck on-line, you should also be getting calls with freight offers. If your own contacts do not result in a load, then move on to the TIA broker list. Be aware there are some days where it is extremely difficult to find a load despite all your efforts. When this is the case, stop calling and continue working your dispatch system again the next day. Over time, you will gain the experience to determine quickly if a load is a "good load" considering all the factors previously discussed. Never simply rely on a broker or agent's word and always follow the proper background and credit check procedure to make sure you are dealing with a financially stable company.

Owner-Operators all over the United States have lost millions of dollars in freight revenue to unscrupulous brokers and shippers.

TruckingSuccess.com has compiled a listing of reliable and ethical brokerage companies that have a good payment history and high credit rating. This listing is included as an appendix to the dispatch manual to help you get started with the understanding that you verify credit ratings and payment history again when you do business with these companies. TruckingSuccess.com cannot guarantee the credit ratings and does not accept legal liability if a company's credit history has changed.

Chapter 6 – Booking Loads

Booking Process

After you verbally agreed via telephone to haul a load and the broker/agent gave you all the pertinent information, you must complete the required paperwork. As stated in Chapter 2, the process of booking a load includes completing a set of legal documents and contracts. When you deal with a brokerage firm for the first time, you have to complete a Vendor Set-up Package, which will be faxed to you, as well as provide information about your business. Your own package of credentials includes a copy of your Carrier Authority issued by the USDOT/FMCSA, a certificate of liability insurance, a completed W-9 form, and several references. You must fax copies of your own credentials along with the completed Vendor Set-up Package to the brokerage firm's designated fax number.

The Vendor Set-up package includes a data sheet that you must complete, the broker/motor carrier agreement (you must place your initials on every page), the brokerage firm's credentials such as a copies of their broker's license issued by the Federal Highway Administration, surety bond certificate, certificate of liability insurance, a blank W-9 form, and credit references. To complete the three-page data sheet, you simply fill in the requested contact information and complete the checklist for required information, and requested information. Usually, the brokerage firm requires that your insurance company include their firm in your insurance certificate as a Certificate Holder.

We advise that you call your insurance company and have them fax the insurance certificate with the name of he Certificate Holder (the brokerage firm) directly to the broker. This will speed up the process of receiving the fax with your rate confirmation sheet signed by the broker. Then, you must sign the rate confirmation sheet and fax it back to the broker (make sure you file the most current rate confirmation sheet because you must submit it later to receive your settlement). Overall, this entire process takes about one to two hours.

If your rate confirmation rate has not arrived after one hours, most likely you are dealing with an unprofessional agent and/or the shipper has not given the okay for the load and the broker wants to hold your truck hoping (s)he gets the load. When you get the impression that the broker/ agent is playing games with you, abandon this load and start searching for another one.

Once you have established business relationships with brokerage companies and/or other logistics companies, the subsequent process of booking loads will be easier and faster because they have your information in their database. After you agreed on a rate for a particular load, the only paperwork involved is the rate confirmation sheet, which the broker/agent will fax to you to sign and then fax it back. Occasionally, circumstances arise that require changes or modifications of the original agreement; e.g., adding lumper fees to the freight rate. Whenever there are changes to the agreed-upon transportation contract, you must request and receive a signed updated rate confirmation sheet because you will be paid according to the information on the rate confirmation sheet.

Credit Check

Before you finalize the booking process, you must complete a credit check to get first-hand information about the company's payment history. Credit services use a rating system to classify a company's creditworthiness. RTS Credit Service uses alphabetical letters A through F to rate a broker's payment history. A rating of A is the best score a company or broker can achieve while a rating of F is the worst score. Brokers with A, B, or C credit ratings are financially stable and pay their bills. Brokers with D, E, or F credit ratings pose a financial risk and you should not do business with them. Even after you have established a business relationship with a shipper or carrier, you should complete a credit check every two to three months to ensure the company's financial stability and payment practices have not deteriorated. In the capital-intensive transportation industry, a company's financial condition can change quickly when a creditor defaults and Owner-Operators cannot afford to not get paid for their services. The six-digit Motor Carrier identification number also provides clues about a company's financial history.

Established companies have lower motor carrier identification numbers; that is, the first three digits of the MC number are in the 100's or 200's such as 101812 or 219322. Companies or brokers with higher Motor Carrier numbers where the first three digits are in the 500's to 700's such as 8 11225 or 954195 are relatively new and may not have established good credit ratings.

Contract Specifics

After you completed all the paperwork involved in booking the load, you must review the contract to ensure it reflects the agreed-upon specifics. Should you discover discrepancies, request a correction of the erroneous information and have an updated rate confirmation sheet and contract faxed to you for your signature.

Freight Rate: This reflects the agreed-upon amount that the Owner-Operator will receive for hauling a particular load. It may also include reimbursements for lumper fees, detention pay, or payment for "deadhead" miles, as well as payment for multiple pick-ups and drops.

Lumper Fees: Federal law states that the shipper is financially responsible for the unloading costs and must reimburse the Owner-Operator for lumping fees. Nowadays, lumping services charge between $80.00 and $140.00 to unload a full trailer. The contract should contain a clause specifying that the Owner-Operator is paid for lumping fees and the method of payment; e.g., by Com-check or reimbursement after the receipt is submitted.

Detention Pay: Federal law does not regulate compensation for waiting time at the loading dock. The prevailing sentiment by regulatory agencies is to let the marketplace sort out how the Owner-Operator is compensated for delays at the loading docks. Nevertheless, most large brokerage companies now pay detention time after a grace period of four to five hours. The industry standard for detention pay is $250.00 for a twenty-four-hour period. It should be a standard clause of every contract of haul. Review your contracts to ensure they contain a clause pertaining to detention pay.

Financial Settlement

Quick Pay: Most brokerage companies offer several payment options including Quick Pay, which means payment is made either within twenty-four hours or seven days after the Owner- Operator submits the signed bill of lading, rate confirmation sheet, and invoice.

Companies offering the service charge a service fee between 3 percent and 5 percent for making the payment within twenty-four hours. For a freight bill of $4,000.00 a 3% fee amounts to $120.00. For payment in seven days, most companies charge a fee of 1% to 2%.

In most cases, the Quick Pay option is listed on the rate confirmation sheet, and the Owner- Operator must check that box to receive Quick Pay as well as note it on the invoice (s)he submits. Some companies require that the Owner-Operator signs up for Quick Pay in advance and then all invoices are processed and paid using the Quick Pay option. Payment is made either with a regular business check mailed to the OwnerOperator's business address or the Owner-Operator can request a Com-check.

Advances: Most companies still offer advances and issue Com-checks to Owner-Operators to cover fuel costs. The amount of the advance depends on the freight rate. Companies charge a 2% fee based on the face amount of the Com-check as well as $25.00 for the cost of the Com-check.

Reimbursements: Most companies issue Com-checks for lumper fees; however, there are exceptions. Some companies require that the Owner-Operator submit the lumper receipts for reimbursement.

Factoring: Factoring companies charge a service fee between 3% to 5% of the freight bill and pay within twenty-four to forty-eight hours after receiving the invoice and required documents. Before you sign up with a factoring service, obtain a sample contract and study the complete document carefully.

Bill of Lading: In order to get paid, the Owner-Operator must submit the bill of lading signed by the receiver, the rate confirmation sheet, and an invoice to the brokerage company. Some companies have specific procedures and designated fax numbers for billings. The Owner-Operator must follow the company's procedure to ensure your paperwork is processed properly and you receive your payment without delay.

Chapter 7 – Freight Handling

Loading

Proper freight handling is a crucial step in the dispatch and transportation chain because the Owner-Operator only receives payment when the freight arrives at its destination on time and without damage. After the freight booking process is completed, the Owner-Operator switches "gears" from being a dispatcher to transportation professional by driving to the designated pickup location, arriving there at the scheduled loading time, and making sure the freight is properly loaded on the trailer.

While at the loading dock, the Owner-Operator must supervise the loading process. That means (s)he must check the paperwork to ensure (s)he picks up the right load because sometimes load numbers get mixed up or the same load number is given to different loads. If there are problems with the load number or other issues arise, the broker must be contacted to clarify the matter. Then (s)he must estimate the total weight by counting the number of pallets and multiplying that number with the weight per pallet to ensure the trailer is not over weight, because there are stiff fines imposed for loads exceeding the maximum weight limit of 80,000 pounds. The Owner-Operator also must instruct the warehouse personnel how to place the pallets on the trailer to ensure proper weight distribution on the axles. That means less-heavy product has to go into the nose of the trailer, the heavier product into the middle section, and less-heavy product again in the tail section. This can be accomplished with the following load distribution pattern: two single, one double, and a single pallet in the trailer nose, the heavier pallets in the middle, and one or two single and one double pallet in the trailer tail. Finally, the total weight must be verified at an official scale.

The Owner-Operator also has to take into consideration that warehouse personnel do not necessarily care about him or her or their truck and trailer. This is a sad but true fact, and forklift operators frequently cause damage to the trailer and/or the product. These careless actions result in costly repairs or deductions from the freight rate; therefore, the Owner-Operator must supervise the loading process and visibly inspect and count the product as it gets loaded onto the trailer to ensure no damage is done to either the product or the trailer or shortages occur.

Securing Shipment

After successfully completing the loading process at the warehouse, the Owner-Operator must secure the freight to prevent damage during transit. Although some minor movement of the product will occur during the transport, significant shifting must be prevented. That means load locks must be installed to keep pallets and product in place, and other required protective material such as airbags must be placed between pallet stacks. Pallet jacks and unused pallets must be secured properly so they do not cause damage to the freight. The trailer must be locked and should not be left unattended for extended periods of time during the transportation process to avoid theft, damage, and pilferage. When the freight consists of high-ticket items, shippers may place a seal on the trailer door; therefore, it is important that the load is secured before the seal is installed.

Refrigerated Product

The Owner-Operator must take extra-special care throughout the entire transportation process when (s)he transports perishable products such as produce, vegetables, and fruit. The Owner-Operator must be familiar with the trailer's refrigeration system to ensure it keeps the trailer and its contents at the required temperature. Temperature checks must be conducted twice a day to verify the "reefer" operates correctly. Prior to loading, the trailer must be inspected for damage to the cooling system, and the integrity of the trailer body verified. Sometimes the air ducts in the ceiling are damaged during loading or unloading, resulting in uneven distribution of cool air in the trailer, which could result in part of the product receiving either not enough or too much refrigeration. Leaks in the trailer's wall, ceiling, or floor may also compromise the effectiveness of the refrigeration system. In either case, the product will spoil and the receiver will reject the shipment, resulting in an insurance claim against the Owner-Operator and (s)he will not receive payment for transportation.

Prior to loading perishable products, the trailer must be pre-cooled for at least thirty minutes and the product must be pre-cooled before loading as well. The Owner-Operator must check the product's temperature to make sure it is not warm when it is brought into the trailer. You must also make sure the trailer doors remain closed before loading and are closed immediately after all product is loaded on the trailer. When you arrive at your destination, you must make sure the product is promptly unloaded after the trailer doors are opened.

Frozen Product

Frozen product must be handled with the same care as refrigerated loads to make sure the product remains frozen and does not spoil. Again, temperature checks must be conducted twice a day to verify the "reefer" operates correctly.

The aforementioned handling instructions for refrigerated and frozen products are general guidelines based on many years of experience hauling refrigerated and frozen loads, and TruckingSuccess.com cannot be held legally liable for product loss. In addition to properly maintaining and servicing the refrigeration unit, the Owner-Operator must follow the operating instructions for the refrigeration equipment (s)he operates and adhere to the shipper's written instructions with regard to product handling.

Chapter 8 – Freight Delivery

Delivery Instructions

In addition to delivery instructions provided by the broker, the Owner-Operator must check the bill of lading for specific instructions and ensure (s)he understands and adheres to the specific requirements such as daily check-in calls and calling ahead to set up a delivery appointment. When daily check-in calls are required, it is important not to miss them and to make the calls at the required time, providing pertinent information about the load to the broker. However, in certain areas of the country cell phones do not work due to a lack of transmission towers, making it difficult to comply with the call-in requirements. In this case, you must call in as soon as you move into an area with cellular reception. It is equally important to call and scheduled the delivery appointment in advance to avoid waiting time and delays at the delivery dock.

Directions, Delays, Troubleshooting

Although routing software and driving direction programs such as Map Quest are available to obtain directions, you should not exclusively rely on these modern technological conveniences because they are not 100% reliable. When you deliver to an unfamiliar location, you should get directions to your delivery destination from the broker and/or receiver. As an Owner-Operator, you must carry in your truck a road atlas designed for the transportation industry and use it to plan the most efficient route to your destination. Detours and delays as a result of "bad" directions waste time, fuel and money. Occasionally, delays are inevitable due to factors beyond the Owner-Operators control. There may be accidents, road construction, or delays due to bad weather. In any case, you should adjust your daily driving schedule to include such delays without impacting your final delivery time.

When the Owner-Operator experiences breakdowns and equipment failure of the truck trailer, the situation becomes more critical and troubleshooting skills are essential to return the equipment into working order and reach the destination in time. The Owner-Operator must have some technical understanding to determine how to handle a breakdown. If it is a relatively minor problem, (s)he may be able to repair or at least temporarily fix the problem in order to get to the next truck stop or repair shop. If it is a major technical problem, a mobile repair service may be able to complete the repair or the truck and trailer may have to be towed. When it becomes obvious that the breakdown will result in a significant delivery delay, the Owner-Operator must contact the broker and advise of the situation so that either a new delivery date may be set or arrange for alternative transportation if there is a risk of product loss.

Delivery & Bill of Lading

The Owner-Operator must arrive at the scheduled delivery time to avoid delays, unnecessary waiting at the dock, and potential rejection of the load. Should (s)he experience excessive delays with unloading nevertheless or other complications at the destination, the broker must be informed immediately about the situation so (s)he can intervene and straighten out the matter. The Owner-Operator must also supervise the unloading process to ensure neither the product nor the trailer are damaged by careless warehouse personnel (please see Chapter 7 for more details), and load locks or other equipment is not stolen. If lumpers are used to unload, the Owner-Operator must obtain a Com-check to pay the fee and a receipt for documentation. In case the Owner-Operator used his or own pallets during the loading process, the pallets must be exchanged.

After the successful completion of the unloading process, the Owner-Operator must obtain a signature on the bill of lading so it can be submitted for payment along with the rate confirmation sheet. Finally, the trailer must be steam-cleaned to avoid possible contamination of the next load.

Rejected Loads

Load rejection is the worst-case scenario of the delivery process and it occurs quite often with produce loads. The load my be rejected for legitimate reasons when the product is spoiled due to improper handling during transit or late delivery; however, many times it appears "games" are being played at the expense of the Owner-Operator and shipper. This can happen when the receiver ordered too much product or does not have enough storage space to unload the product. Regardless of the circumstances, when it appears a load is being rejected, the Owner-Operator must be vigilant to ensure no tampering with the load occurs, such as pulling pallets off the truck and letting them sit at the dock, and the broker must be notified immediately. Also, the federal inspector must be notified to inspect the product and issue an inspection report.

Appendix

Brokerage Companies By State, Recommended on the Basis of Years in Business and By Credit Ratings:

The Brokerage Firms Pay Between 10 and 30 days after Receipt of BOL and they also have Advances and Quick Pay Options Available.

Before accepting a load check your cost per mile, don't pay the broker and haul cheap loads.

Alabama

G & P Distributing, Inc., Albertville, AL P: 800-374-3067 F:256-891-9764 loads from GA to west coast

C2 Freight Resources, Houston, AL P: 888-371-5335 F: 205-489-5326 loads from OH to TX.

McAlpin Transportation, Inc., Vinemont, AL P: 877-253-4457 F: 256-739-9390 loads in 48 states, Canada and Mexico.

Arizona

Best Freight, LLC, Buckeye, AZ   P: 623-386-4266 F: 623-386-4571 loads from TX or east coast to AZ - loads from AZ to 48 states -loads from north west to AZ.

Crossroad Transportation, Mesa, AZ   P: 800-777-9830 F:480-991-5740 loads in 48 states and out of west coast.

Bigelow Truck Brokers, Inc. Glendale, AZ P: 623-931-5955 F: 623-931-7131 loads from AZ to east coast and 11 western states.

All American Carriers, Glendale, AZ P: 623-842-4460 F: 623-842-4539 loads from CA to east and east to west.

Freightmatchers.com, Glendale, AZ P: 602-237-6718
F: 623-321-9288 loads from CA to 48 states.

Greenway Transportation Service, Inc. Scottsdale, AZ P: 800-528-4025 and   480-443-8800 Fax: 480-998-9440 - loads from AZ to east coast.

Advantage Transport, Phoenix, AZ P: 800-444-0808 and 602-331-0808 F: 800-516-0975 loads from 11 western states and south east and northeast.

Arkansas   - ABF Freight, Fort Smith, AR P: 877-279-8090

F: 479-494-81 loads from north east to south east.
Willis Shaw Express, Inc., Elm Springs, AR P: 877-405-1298
F: 479-248-1967 loads from 48 states.
Stallion Transportation Group, Beebe, AR P: 800-597-2425
F: 501-882-1588 loads from 48 states
Jerry Dudley, Inc., Fayettsville, AR
800-221-0723 loads from DE to CA -US-Mail – loads from IL to 48 states.
Addison Transportation, Cabot, AR
P: 800-580-6560   F: 501-843-7279 loads from 48 states.
BNSF Logistics LLC, Springdale, AR P: 800-941-0724
F:479-587-7254 loads from east to west.

California

Allen Lund Company, Inc., La Canada, CA   P: 800-777-6142
F:800-434-5863 loads from 48 states.

RLT, Inc. Redding, CA   P: 800-824-4121   F: 530-241-7084
loads from Nogales, AZ to WA, OR, CA

Bowers Trucking, Oroville, CA P: 800-821-0545
F: 530-534-8878 loads from 48 states.

LLR Logistics, LLC, Monrovia, CA   P: 866-236-2275   F: 626-447-0294
loads from IA to UT.

American Freightways, San Diego, CA
P: 866-326-5902   F: 858-217-3305 loads from CA to east coast.

Cargo Master, Inc., Lake Elsinore, CA   P: 800-683-750

Diversified Transportation Services, Torrance, CA P: 800-460-8540
F: 310-436-1970 loads from 48 states and international.

Colorado

CR England, Greeley, CO   P: 800-321-5966   F: 970-330-4500
loads from TX to CO.

Timberline Freight Service, Evergreen, CO   P: 1-800-495-9102
F: 303-674-9104 loads from OK-TX-Panhandle to west
and north-west 17 states.

Olathe Trucking, LLC, Denver, CO
P: 888-627-0121   F: 303-573-0663 loads from CO to 11 western
states.

Freight Logistics, Inc., Denver, CO
800-575-3346
F:720-377-9463 loads from 48 states.

Connecticut

United Express Service, Inc., Rocky Hill, CT P: 860-529-7737 F: 860-721-7737 loads from 48 states.

Delaware

Trinity Transport, Inc., Seaford, DE -loads 48 states. P: 800-846-3400

Florida

John Green Logistics, Titusville, FL P: 800-538-5984 F: 321-269-2340 loads out of FL to 48 states.

All-Ways Transport, Inc., Saint Petersburg, FL 800-851-8801 F: 727-821-0188 loads from FL to 48 states.

Astra, Inc., Plantation, FL P: 800-881-8123 F:954-583-5778 LTL loads from FL to 48 states.

Intermodal Logistics, Inc., Miami, FL P:800-766-7778 F: 305-670-9776 loads from FL to 48 states.

Georgia

**Trans Dynamics, Norcross, GA P: 800-827-7717
F: 770-921-4482 loads from GA to west coast.**

**Freight Shakers USA Inc., Stockbridge, GA P: 800-894-8383
F: 770-507-9713 loads from GA to mid west.**

**Scott Logistics Corp., Rome, GA P: 800-893-6689
F: 706-234-9141 loads from GA to MD and NJ**

**DSL, Inc. Smyrna, GA , P: 1-800-267-1370 F: 770-980-9770
loads from MI to CO and west coast.**

**American Transp. Systems, Inc., Tucker, GA P: 800-888-2874
F: 706-561-7533 loads from GA to TX.**

**GTO 2000, Inc., Gainesville, GA, P: 800-966-0801 F: 770-287-7878
loads from 48 states.**

Illinois

Henderson Trucking, Salem, IL P: 800-851-4943
F: 618-548-1913 loads from FL to CA.

ADM Logistics, Inc., Decatur, IL   P: 800-637-5843 F: 217-451-3278
loads from 48 states.

Sunshine Logistics Inc., Melrose Park, IL
P: 708-216-0200 F: 708-216-0206 loads from 48 states.

Freight Flow, Ltd., Bloomingdale, IL
P: 800-752-1202 F: 630-307-7400 loads from 48 states.

Seal Transportation, Inc., Hoffman Estates, IL
P: 800-373-2977 F: 847-884-7300 IL to 48 states.

Indiana

All Points Logistics, Inc., Indianapolis, IN   P: 317-544-1484
F: 317-544-1472 loads from 48 states.

Iowa

Ruan Transport Corp., Des Moines, IA

P: 800-493-0810 F: 515-558-3901 loads from CA and KS to west and east coast.

Norseman Transportation, Inc., Lake Mills, IA
800-284-8413 F: 847-599-3070 loads from FL to mid west.

Pioneer Transfer, LLC Sioux City, IA
800-325-712-2946 loads from NJ to FL.

Kansas

All Freight Brokerage, Kansas City, KS
P: 800-793-7933   F: 913-281-3338 loads from CA to mid west.

Coast to Coast Transportation Inc., Emporia, KS

P: 620-342-2407 F: 620-342-3128 Loads from 48 states.

Mid-America Brokers, Kansas City, KS
P: 800-279-9142 F: 816-471-5723 loads from KS to CA.

GS Enterprises, Kansas City, KS
P: 1-877-631-1254 F: 913-543-7625 loads from CA to AZ.

Kentucky

J & J Transportation, Inc., Louisville, KY
P: 800-548-7488 F: 502-266-5176 loads from VA to west coast.

Louisiana

Cargo Master Inc., Natchitoches, LA   P: 800-683-8750
F: 318-357-1732 Loads from 48 states.

Maine

ET Transportation, Palermo, ME

P: 800-940-1596 F: 207-993-2839 loads from GA to ME.

North Star Transport Group Inc., Scarborough, ME
800-266-9586   F: 207-885-9816 Loads from 48 states.

Maryland

Choptank Transport Inc., Preston, MD
P: 800-568-2240 F: 410-673-2835 loads from NJ, PA to nationwide.

Atlantic Transportation Services, Inc., Rosedale, MD
800-477-8159 F: 410-406-8114 Loads from 48 states.

Massachusetts

RFX Inc., Avon, MA P: 800-342-8822 F: 508-583-3900 loads from MA and NJ to TX and west.

Allen Lund Company – Boston, MA P: 800-381-5863
F: 800-237-1622 loads from northeast to CA.

All States Transport Inc., Springfield, MA
P: 800-979-9599 F: 413-739-3758 Loads from 48 states.

Michigan

VSF Transportation, Inc., Wyoming, MI
P: 800-445-5623 F: 616-530-4902 loads from AZ to CA and 48 states.

RCT, Inc., Wayland, MI   P: 800-677-2022 F: 616-662-2435 loads from MI to NC.

Total Logistic Control, LLC, Zeeland, MI
P: 888-788-3285 F: 616-772-9903 loads from S. California to IL.

Cornerstone Systems, Grand Rapids, MI
P: 800-856-7872 F: 616-791-4040 loads from CA to NH and FL.

Minnesota

Traffic Management Inc., Minneapolis, MN
P: 888-726-9559 F: 763-544-3458 loads from 48 states.

Wagoneer Transportation, Inc., Eden Prairie, MN P: 800-278-0050
F: 952-833-3024 loads from OH to AZ and CA.

Online Freight Services, Inc., Mendota Heights, MN 800-284-2603
F:651-468-6869 loads from FL to west coast.

Bartels Transportation Services, Inc., Winthrop, MN P: 800-422-1347
F: 612-395-9116 Loads from 48 states.

Missouri

Prime Inc, Springfield, MO
P: 800-498-9268 F: 417-521-6876 loads from mid west
or north east to CA.

Coastal Carriers, Inc., Troy, MO P: 877-848-8726
F: 636-528-5879 loads from CA to east
coast.

UTXL, Inc., Kansas City, MO   P: 800-351-2821 or 816-383-2638
loads from OH to west coast.

Nightline Express Inc., Saint Louis, MO
P: 800-317-9333 F: 314-416-1660 Loads from 48 states.

Ortran, Inc., Independence, MO
P: 816-373-8855 F: 816-373-8897 Loads from 48 states.

Montana

Freight Agency Inc., Billings, MT P: 800-676-6166
F: 406-245-5404 Loads from 48 states.

DTS Logistics, Billings, MT   P: 406-896-3460
F: 406-896-3490
loads from MS to west coast.

Nebraska

Grand Island Express, Grand Island, NE P: 1-800-444-9008
F: 308-384-7672 loads from IN to CO

United Dispatch Inc., Omaha, NE P: 800-228-9272
F: 402-330-5617 Loads from NE to 48 states.

New York

Trans-Pro, Champlain, NY   P: 800-463-7532
F:866-358-9203
loads from east coast to 48 states. Also loads from
CA

T.F.G. Transport, LLC, Canandaigua, NY
P: 800-396-1832   F: 585-919-0059 loads from NY to CA and to TX,
LA
IL.

Productive Transportation Services, Tonawanda, NY 800-777-5656
F: 716-877-6331 loads from NY to west coast.

Trailer Transport System, Inc., Rochester, NY
P: 585-427-2080   F: 585-427-0559 loads from NY State to West.

Logistic Dynamics, Amherst, NY
P: 800-554-3734   F: 716-250-3498 loads from MA and NH to VA.

North Carolina

Bradco Transp., Inc., Graham, NC P: 336-578-0193
F:336-578-9026 loads from MI to GA.

Wootton Transportation, Durham, NC
P: 800-222-4751 F: 919-688-2635 loads from NJ to south east.

Salem Logistics, Inc., Winston Salem, NC P: 800-326-5268
F:336-725-5123 Loads from 48 states.

New Jersey

Genpro Transportation Services, Newark, NJ   800-243-6770
F: 973-589-1877 loads from AZ to east coast.

Paramount Freight Systems, Inc., Lodi, NJ P: 800-590-6642
F: 201-462-0507 loads from NJ to west coast.

Amodei Brokerage Co., Marlton, NJ P: 800-266-3341
F: 856-874-9240 loads from NJ to west coast.

North Dakota

Land Transportation, LLC, Fargo, ND
P: 800-437-4166 F: 701-282-9760 loads from NJ, PA to west coast.

Davis Trucking Inc., Jamestown, ND 888-252-5831
F:701-252-0282 load from PA to west coast.

Britton Transport, Inc., Grand Forks, ND P: 701-772-6681
F: 701-746-6493 loads from east coast to west.

Ohio

Total Quality Logistics, Inc., Milford, OH - 800-580-3101 - loads from 48 states.

BNSF Logistics, LLC, OH, P: 800-766-6870 F: 618-466-3095 loads from 48 states.

Logan Logistics LLC, Canton, OH P: 800-821-7054 F:330-478-0557 loads from OH to CA.

Bridge Logistics, Cincinnati, OH   P: 800-522-0671 F:513-874-4161 loads from MA to west coast.

MCS – Motor Carrier Service, Northwood, Ohio - P: 800-359-9710 loads from OH to MO.

Fleet Service, Inc., Newark, OH
P: 800-999-7566 loads from OH to CA.

Oklahoma

Mark Westby & Associates, Inc., Tulsa, OK 918-632-0010 F: 918-632-0030 loads from MI -OH -PA to southeast.

D&M Carriers, Inc., Oklahoma City, OK
P: 800-645-4084 loads from CO to east coast.

Smart Lines, Oklahoma City, OK
P: 866-865-4637 F: 405-848-2960 loads from OK and mid west to 48 states.

Oregon

I.C.C.I., Medford, OR   P: 800-422-8785 F: 541-734-9142
loads from CA to OR and WA

Intransit Inc., Medford, OR   P: 1-800-547-2053 F: 541-770-1399
loads from IL, MO, OR, WA to TX

K & M Distribution, Rogue River, OR P: 800-221-0182
F:541-582-1450 loads from OR and CA to east
coast.

Beaver Freight Services, LLC, Portland, OR P: 800-800-2066
F:503-281-4773 loads from CO to east coast.

Hammell Logistics, Hermiston, OR P: 866-314-8997
F: 541-567-7607 loads from VA to west coast.

Interstate Logistics Inc., Portland, OR P: 800-860-2322
F:503-240-6303 loads from CA to OR.

Integrity Logistics, Beaverton, OR P: 503-582-4444
F:503-582-4445 loads from WA to CA.

Truck Transportation Services, Wilsonville, OR
P: 800-632-0228 loads from OR to east coast.

Northland Express Transport, Troutdale,
OR P 800-950-1010 loads from OR to East.

Hammell Logistics, Inc., Hermiston, OR
P: 866-314-8997 loads from FL to CA.

Truck Transportation Services, Wilsonville,
OR P: 800-632-0228 loads from OR to NC.

Pennsylvania

Mawson & Mawson Inc., Langhorne, PA P: 800-262-9766 F:215-750-7835 loads from NJ and PA to west coast.

Trans 58, Edinboro, PA P: 800-685-7671 F:814-734-8920 loads from PA to TX.

JR Transportation, Lancaster, PA P: 800-462-6049 F: 717-394-1600 loads from NJ to TN.

Action Cargo Freight, Hanover Township, PA P: 800-451-3158 F: 866-815-8767 loads from 48 states.

South Carolina

Gene Morris Co, Inc., Columbia, SC P: 800-232-4363 F: 803-419-5558 loads from GA to South west.

South Dakota

MCT Logistics LLC., Sioux Falls, SD P: 605-339-8400 F: 605-339-8449 loads from OH to TX.

Tennessee

ATS Logistics Services Inc., Brentwood, TN P: 800 338-0497 F:615-373-5384 Loads from 48 states.

Truckload Carriers of Chattanooga, LLC, Chattanooga, TN 800-785-8664 F: 423-894- 4550—loads from 48 states.

Cornerstone Systems, Inc., Memphis, TN P: 800-278-7677 F: 901-842-0675 Loads from 48 states.

Texas

MTS Transportation Inc., Amarillo, TX P: 806-622-8400
806-622-8408 loads from Texas and Greeley CO to CA

Bertling Logistics, Inc., Houston, TX   P: 800-846-8743
F:713-490-9235 loads from TX to 48 states and inside CA.

A&A Transportation, San Antonio, TX   P: 800-367-0294
F:210-568-8907 loads from South TX to 48 states.

Bear Transportation Services, Dallas, TX P: 800-527-5380
F:972-239-6321 loads from TX to 48.

Cargo-Master, Inc., Dallas, TX   P: 800-683-8750 F: 214-428-3604
loads from TX to west coast.

Amino Transport, Inc. Hurst, TX - P: 800-842-7251
F: 817-514-3803 loads from TX to AZ.

Heyl Logistics, Edinburg, TX - P: 800-292-6778
F: 956-383-0319 loads from South Texas to CA.

Stevens Transport, Dallas, TX P: 800-347-4312 F: 502-839-8572
loads from TX to west coast.

Allen Lund, San Antonio, TX   P: 800-456-5863   F: 800-477-5863
loads from TX to CO and west coast.

Swan Transportation, Tyler, TX P: 903-533-4086 F: 903-533-9742
loads from North TX, OK to east coast.

Logistic Services, Richmond, TX P: 800-214-9660
F: 832-595-8239 loads from south east to TX.

Mason Haulers, Pearland, TX   P: 866-304-3064   F: 817-545-7510   and
F: 281-992-6709 - loads from AL to west coast.

Federal Transportation Systems, Inc., Houston, TX P: 800-231-0245
F:713-464-4671 Loads from 48 states and Mexico.

Elston Nationwide Carriers, Hurst, TX P: 800-288-4314
F:817-427-1007 loads from TX to 48 states.

JKC Enterprises, Mansfield, TX - P: 800-783-8565   F: 817-842-4210
loads from OH to TX.

Blakeman Transportation, Fort Worth, TX P: 800-375-9995

GTO 2000, Inc., Salt Lake City, UT   P: 866-558-3495   F: 702-564-8623
loads from CO and NV to TX and from AZ to CA. (office moved to
Henderson NV)

Central Refrigerated Service, Inc., West Valley City,
UT P: 800-777-9100 F: 801-924-7131 -loads from OH
to CA and CO to CA.

Cargo Master Inc, Clearfield, UT P: 800-683-8750
F:801-773-9326 Loads from 48 states.

Virginia

**Allstate Transport Services, Fredericksburg, VA P: 540-752-9698
F: 540-752-9356 Loads from 48 states.**

Washington

**Kader Co., Yakima, WA   P: 509-248-2777   F: 509-575-4942
loads from WA and OR to east coast –**

**Shippers Choice Transportation Services, Wenatchee, WA P: 800-323-8103
F: 509-663-8736 loads from 48 states.**

**Gulick Freight Services Logistics, Vancouver, WA P: 877-470-0971
F: 360-695-4787 loads from OR, WA to east coast.**

**Allen Lund, Washington State   P: 800-999-5863   F: 360-256-4080 loads
from WA and OR to east coast.**

**Blackhorse Transportation Group, Silverdale, WA
P: 800-800-7136   F: 360-638-0874 loads from WA , OR to east coast.**

**Associated Freight Brokers, Yakima, WA   P: 800-548-0669
509-575-6555 loads from TX to west coast.**

Wisconsin

Elite Freight Solutions LLC, Manitowoc, WI   P: 920-686-8200 F: 920-682-3097 loads from OR and CA to east coast.

M2 Logistics Inc., Green Bay, WI P: 920-569-8801 F: 920-569-8843 Loads from 48 states.

Northern Freight Service, Inc., Middleton, WI P: 800-383-8688 F: 608-836-4070 Loads from 48 states.

TruckingSuccess.com

7054 North 28th Drive
Phoenix, AZ 85051
Tel. (602) 864-8056
support@truckingsuccess.com

*Information presented in this brochure is current at the time of printing.
Specifications subject to change.*
TXu1-335-556
Copyright 2020 TruckingSuccess.com All Rights Reserved.

The Successful Truck Owner Operator

2020 EDITION

**A Business Guide
For The Start-Up
Independent Owner Operator**

The Successful Truck Owner Operator

A BUSINESS MANUAL FOR THE INDEPENDENT Start-UP OWNER OPERATOR

BY J.W. LESSING

Table of Contents

Chapter 1 Getting Started
Economic Outlook
New HOS Regulations
CSA 2010
CDL

Chapter 2 Business Structures
Sole Proprietorship
Partnership
Corporations / LLC

Chapter 3 Buying your Truck
Financial Aspects
Selecting a Used Truck
Maintenance & Repair

Chapter 4 Operating Authority
Leasing On
Negotiating a Lease
Own Authority

Chapter 5 Business Records
Maintaining Records
Cash Management
Cost-Per-Mile Calculation

Chapter 6 Registration & Taxes
Vehicle Registration
Fuel & Road Taxes
Log Book - Trip Sheet
ELD Regulations

Introduction

Dear Trucking Partner:

Congratulations on your decision to start your own business in the trucking industry. The success of the American economy depends on enterprising men and women like you who make their living in this field.

The independent truck owner-operator faces a unique and challenging business environment as (s)he conducts business on the open road from a truck that not only serves as an office, but also as a second home.

Motivation and hard work alone will not guarantee success. You have to possess business skills, technical knowledge and industry experience to succeed as an owner-operator.

Our business manual will guide you through the process of getting started in trucking. Then it will show you how to develop a business plan and how to successfully manage your day-to-day operations. Finally, it will explain why and how you can obtain your own operating authority.

Thank you for choosing our publication "The Successful Truck Owner Operator."

Best wishes for a successful future,

J.W. Lessing

Getting Started

Trucks transport 94 percent of all consumer, 77 percent of all industrial, and 68 percent of all farm goods in the United States, according to the U.S. Department of Transportation. Annually, the value of all goods shipped exceeds $6 trillion.

You are excited about your career decision, but please proceed with caution and prudence. Owning and operating an 18-wheeler requires research and planning.

As an owner-operator, you make sacrifices because your business requires you to work nights, on weekends and even holidays, often away from your family.

Good preparation and careful consideration of what makes an owner- operator successful will help you avoid costly mistakes that can set you back or even destroy your dream.

Such a major decision affects you, your spouse and your family. Include them in your decision-making process, since your family's support will contribute to your success.

Begin with a thorough self- assessment of your skills and experience. Then list your strengths and weaknesses. This exercise will improve your self-awareness and decision making.

Use this list as your guide:
- Years of driving experience - Crisis management
- Trucking-related skills - Motivation and endurance
- Mechanical skills - Willingness to learn
- Basic business experience - Stress management
- Money management skills - Flexibility
- Basic bookkeeping - Willingness to sacrifice
- Computer skills - Familiar with Internet
- Communication style
- Other experience

The Economic Outlook for 2020

The Economic Outlook for 2020. The trucking industry's fortunes falls and rises with the American economy. At this time, the outlook for 2020 is courteous optimistic and industry experts expect a slow but steady recovery of the economic growth experienced in 2019 will continue into next year. For 2020, a growth rate in the 3.5 - 5% range in the first quarter of 2020 is anticipated. Predicting the heavy truck market for 2020 is showing the same improvements like the 3rd quarter of 2019.

There are just so many variables in the equations. Many we can make educated guesses about. The big one though, the overall health of the economy is improving and therefore can give us a clue about 2020.

After dropping earlier in 2017 and in 2018, the Truck Tonnage Index is up 6.7%, and the long-term outlook for 2020 will see some moderate gains for the 1st and 2nd half of 2020. The reduction in supply since the start of the recession means that even small improvements in tonnage will have a larger impact on the industry than in the past. The shortage of qualified drivers, particularly in the long-haul sector, could become a long term problem. Despite the favorable outlook for 2020 with regard to capacity and revenue, carriers as well as Owner-Operators will still have to tightly control costs. A decrease in fuel prices and slightly improved growth in freight volume may drive financially stable carriers and Owner-Operators to expand their business.

> One other silver-lining is the congressional interest in energy and environmental matters.
> Mandate a fuel surcharge pass-through to the person who bought the fuel.
> A measure designed to protect independents and

small fleet operators. The fuel surcharge belongs in the owners pocket, not in the brokers pocket.

At this time we can't predict the cross border capacity because President Donald Trump has renegotiated NAFTA with Canada and Mexico.

International trade and exports, particularly with Mexico and Canada, may contribute to economic growth and increase capacity because most cross-border freight moves by truck. Nevertheless, the freight markets will fall and rise according to seasonal demand as well as economic cycles. As always, the fall and pre-holiday months are busy, followed by a slowdown beginning inthe middle of December and lasting through March because there is less consumer demand. During seasons of peak demand, capacity will be tight. Since there is more demand than supply, larger carriers will be able to raise freight rates and shippers may be willing to pay premium rates to move undesirable freight and perishable goods. However, high fuel costs add to operating costs and may offset higher revenue, thereby limiting profitability. Nevertheless, Owner operators might have more freight to haul in 2020 and might benefit from higher rates.

The revised Hours of Service regulations which went into effect on January 4, 2004, is in effect. These rules are implemented in the new CSA 2010 regulations.

Fuel prices have not had such a devastating effect on the trucking industry as in past years.

Fuel surcharges have helped carriers deal with increased fuel costs; however, when fuel costs rise quickly, the surcharge does not always cover the in-crease. Although fuel prices went up from the national average of $2.50 in June 2019 to $3.40 in November 2019, industry experts believe fuel prices will remain at about $2.95-$3.25 in 2020.

With fuel being the #1 expense, Owner-Operators will have to continue monitoring fuel usage and plan their fuel stops to avoid having to fuel up in states where prices are high. Regional differences in fuel prices affect the Owner- Operator's profitability. The West Coast, Southwest and the Midwest have the highest regional average prices, at $3.65 to $3.85 per gallon. Fuel is more reasonable in the South and the Western Mountain regions at $3.20 to $3.40 per gallon average. Up and down the East Coast, the regional average is $3.60 per gallon.

Overall, insurance rates will remain high in 2020, particularly workers' compensation and health insurance. However, premiums for liability and cargo insurance are leveling off due to increased competition among insurers. Still, an Owner Operator can expect to pay between $7,000 and $10,000 a year for general liability insurance.

Truckers with a good safety record may see premium reductions, and there is an expectation that premiums will come down. Nevertheless, with low interest rates, it may be cheaper to borrow the money and earn a discount by paying the annual premium in one lump sum, rather than financing it through the insurance provider. To lower insurance costs, Owner Operators may raise deductibles and pay out of pocket for small claims.

Interest rates have dropped to historically low levels in recent years and are expected to remain low as the Federal Reserve continues to manage the economic expansion.

However, lower interest rates do not automatically translate into cheap financing for buying equipment. Lenders continue to limit their best deals to buyers with excellent credit because they still consider trucking a high credit risk due to the significant rate of business failures in previous years. Start- ups will have difficulty finding affordable financing, especially if they have little cash to invest.

If you're in need of financing and you're credit rating is rather low or not that good, please go to our website www.truckingsuccess.com and consider an SBA loan by using our business plan trucking.

The huge inventories of used trucks is even bigger now, the Owner-Operator going into business now can find a nice selection of used trucks at low prices, according to the *American Trucker* magazine.

Many dealers offer their inventories on the Internet, and prospective buyers can do comparison shopping on-line. Additionally, manufacturer-owned finance companies will offer attractive interest rates to qualified buyers to help move trucks.

The man or woman who owns and operates an 18-wheeler must have multiple talents. In addition to excellent driving and road skills, the successful owner-operators qualities include:

Communication skills. In the course of a day, the owner-operator may speak with dispatchers, shippers, DOT inspectors and the highway patrol. To succeed, she-he must think, speak and act like a business owner, choosing an appropriate communication style to fit the occasion.

Business skills. The owner-operator works hard and uses many resources to succeed. She-he applies sound business principles and keeps accurate records.

She-he uses the internet in the day-to-day management of the business to find loads, obtain licensing/toll information, directions, the best routes and road conditions, to ensure the load gets to the destination on time.

Solid Decision-making Skills.
The owner-operator knows the operating costs and uses the cost per mile calculation in order to accept good paying loads and he/she knows what route to travel.

Mechanical aptitude. Down times and expensive truck repairs eat into the profit margin. The owner- operator must have an understanding of the truck's systems and components and how they work together so (s)he can perform small repairs and deal with emergency situations on the road.

Please do not feel discouraged if you fall short on the list of skills and experience. You have one important skill: the capacity to learn. Take the time now, before you start driving your big rig, to acquire and develop the skills that will contribute to your success!

The Revised Hours-Of-Service Regulations

On January 4, 2004, the Revised Hours-Of-Service Regulations went into effect and the Federal Motor Carrier Safety Administration (FMCSA) and its state enforcement partners began enforcing the final rule on that date. Despite recent court challenges, carriers, independent truckers, and Owner Operators are required to operate under these new rules.

In April 2003, the FMCSA issued the first significant revision to the Hours-Of-Service (HOS) regulations since 1939 when the original HOS rules were prescribed for truckers.

Concerns about the effect of fatigue as a contributing factor in commercial motor vehicle (CMV) crashes and new scientific findings related to driver fatigue and sleep disorder research led to the new rule-making.

The FMCSA had considered re- forming the HOS regulations for some time. However, in 1995 Congress directed the FMCSA to begin rule making on new HOS regulations that increase driver alertness and reduce fatigue-related incidents.

According to the FMCSA, the revised regulations' primary benefit is an increased opportunity for drivers to obtain needed rest and restorative sleep while reflecting the operational realities of motor carrier transportation. The new rules will improve highway safety and help reduce the number of commercial truck crashes and related deaths and injuries.

The new rules govern drivers transporting freight in interstate commerce in a property carrying commercial vehicle with a gross weight rating of 10,001 pounds or more, and

operating vehicles transporting hazardous materials in quantities requiring vehicle placards. Rules for the record-of- duty status form, which is commonly referred to as the driver's daily log, (now ELD) remain unchanged for truck drivers.

The following is a summary of the new HOS rules' main points:

- Daily Cycle: 10 hours off and 14 hours on.
- On Duty: The 14 consecutive hours on duty include breaks. Local drivers may extend this to 16 hours one day a week
- under certain circumstances.

- <u>Driving Time</u>: 11 hours.
- <u>Off Duty</u>: 10 consecutive hours.
- <u>Breaks</u>: Breaks during duty time (on duty) are discretionary.
- <u>Weekly Hours</u>: If the company does not run trucks daily, a driver may not drive after 60 hours logged "on-duty" in 7 consecutive days. If the company runs trucks daily, a driver may not drive after 70 hours logged "on-duty" in ay period of 8 consecutive days. Time logged as "off-duty" is not counted in calculating "on-duty" time.
- <u>Weekly Break</u>: At least 34 consecutive hours (1 day 10 hours).
- <u>Restart</u>: A break of 34 consecutive hours "restarts" the weekly cycle.

- <u>Sleeper Berth</u>: Among the changes in the 2005 rules, perhaps the most significant and most confusing relates to the split-sleeper option. That is the option that allows a driver to split his/her required 10 consecutive hours of rest into two separate, non-consecutive breaks. Though the split-sleeper option will still be an option after October 1st, for both teams and individual drivers, the requirements will change significantly so much, in fact, that many are wondering if they should continue using the option at all.

Under the 2003 rules, a driver could split his/her time into any combination of two breaks that added up to 10 hours, so long as the breaks were at least 2 hours long. These breaks had to be spent entirely in the berth, but they were excluded from the 14- hour limit.

Under the 2005 rules, you still need two breaks that add up to 10 hours. But, recognizing that drivers need 7 to 8 hours of continuous sleep to beat fatigue, the rules require one of the two breaks to be at least 8 continuous hours. Like the 2003 rules, this break must be spent entirely in the sleeper berth, and it will still be excluded from the 14-hour limit.

The other break must be at least 2 hours long (this is so that the driver gets the required 10 total hours of rest), but this break can be spent off duty, in the sleeper berth, or any combination of the two. In addition, this shorter break is always included in the 14-hour limit, no matter where it is spent (i.e., it always counts against the driver, even if it is spent in the sleeper berth). Because one of the two breaks will count against the driver's 14-hour limit, the new rules change the way you calculate available hours after a break. As under the 2003 rules, once you have completed two qualifying rest breaks that add up to 10 hours (one being at least 8 hours in a sleeper berth), you do not gain back a full 11 driving hours and 14 on-duty hours.

Rather, following the second rest break, hours available under the 11 and 14 hour rules must be recalculated from the end of the first of the two breaks.

Examples: Suppose driver Smith takes 10 hours off and starts driving. He drives for 6 hours and then decides to take a 2-hour nap. Those 2 hours will count against his 14 hour limit no matter where he takes them (off duty and/or sleeper). After his nap, he drives for his remaining 5 hours and is then at hour 13 out of 14 (6+2+5=13). To gain time back, Smith may either: Go off duty and/or in the sleeper for 10 consecutive hours; or go into the sleeper berth for only 8 hours. If he chooses to take 10 hours off, he will gain a full 11 and 14 hours. Suppose he chooses an 8 hour sleeper berth. How much driving and on-duty time does he have remaining at the end of that break? We start counting from the end of the first break (the 2 hour nap), and arrive at the following numbers:

Driving time: 11−5 hours driving after the 2 hour nap − 6 hours remaining.

Duty time: 14−5 hours spent after the 2 hour nap = 9 hours remaining.

Driver Smith starts driving again.

Suppose he uses his remaining 6 hours of driving time, has another 2 hours on duty (not driving), and wants to return to driving. At this point, he has used up his 11 hours of driving time and is at hour 13 of 14 available.

Drivers or carriers who violate the Hours-Of-Service regulations, face the following penalties:

- Drivers may be placed out of service (shut down) at roadside until the driver has accumulated enough off-duty time to be back in compliance;
- State and local enforcement officials may assess fines;

Hours of Service for Drivers, effective July 1, 2013

AGENCY: Federal Motor

Carrier Safety

Administration (FMCSA),

ACTION: Final rule.

SUMMARY: FMCSA revises the hours of service (HOS) regulations to limit the use of the 34- hour restart provision to once every 168 hours and to require that anyone using the 34- hour restart provision have as part of the restart two periods that include 1 a.m. to 5 a.m.

It also includes a provision that allows truckers to drive if they have had a break of at least 30 minutes, at a time of their choosing, sometime within the previous 8 hours. This rule does not include a change to the daily driving limit because the Agency is unable to definitively demonstrate that a 10-hour limit which it favored in the notice of proposed rule making (NPRM) would have higher net benefits than an 11-hour limit. The current 11- hour limit is therefore unchanged at this time.

The 60- and 70-hour limits are also unchanged. The purpose of the rule is to limit the ability of drivers to work the maximum number of hours currently allowed, or close to the maximum, on a continuing basis to reduce the possibility of driver fatigue.

Long daily and weekly hours are associated with an increased risk of crashes and with the chronic health conditions associated with lack of sleep. These changes will affect only the small minority of drivers who regularly work the longer hours.

Compliance date: The rule changes that affect Appendix B to Part 386 Penalty Schedule; Violations and Monetary Penalties; the oilfield exemption in § 395.1(d)(2); and the definition of on-duty time in § 395.2 must be complied with on the effective date. Compliance for all the other rule changes is not required until December 18, 2017.

The Commercial Driver's License

Since April 1, 1992, the Federal Motor Carrier Safety Administration (**FMCSA**) has required drivers to possess a Commercial Driver's License (**CDL**) to operate commercial motor vehicles (**CMV**).

A driver must take the CDL test in his/her home state and cannot hold more than one commercial driver's license. The CDL replaced and invalidated previously issued chauffeur licenses.

Driving CMV's requires special skills and knowledge. Prior to implementation of the CDL Program, in a number of states and the District of Columbia, any person licensed to drive an automobile could also legally drive a tractor-trailer or a bus. Even in many of the states that did have a classified licensing system, a person was not skills tested in a representative vehicle. Many drivers were operating motor vehicles that they may not have been qualified to drive, and were able to obtain driver's licenses from more than one state and hide or spread convictions among several driving records and continue to drive.

The **Commercial Motor Vehicle Safety Act of 1986** was signed into law on October 27, 1986, with the goal to improve highway safety by ensuring that drivers of large trucks and buses are qualified to operate those vehicles and to remove unsafe and unqualified drivers from the highways. The Act retained the state's right to issue a driver's license, but established minimum national standards which states must meet when licensing CMV drivers.

> The Act corrects the situation existing prior to 1986 by making it illegal to hold more than one license and by requiring states to adopt testing and licensing standards for truck and bus drivers to check a person's ability to operate the type of vehicle (s)he plans to operate.

The Act does not require drivers to obtain a separate Federal license. It merely required states to upgrade their existing testing and licensing programs, if necessary, to conform with the Federal minimum standards.

The CDL places requirements on the CMV driver, the employing motor carrier and the states. The FHWA has developed and issued standards for testing and licensing CMV drivers. Among other things, the standards require States to issue CDL's to their CMV drivers only after a driver passes knowledge and skills tests administered by the state related to the type of vehicle to be operated. Drivers need CDL's if they are in interstate, intrastate, or foreign commerce and drive a vehicle that meets one of the following definitions of a CMV. The Federal standard requires states to issue a CDL to drivers according to the following licensing classifications:

Class A — Any combination of vehicles with a GCWR of 26,001 or more pounds provided the GVWR of the vehicle(s) being towed is in excess of 10,000 pounds.

Class B — Any single vehicle with a GVWR of 26,001 or more pounds, or any such vehicle towing a vehicle not in excess of 10,000 pounds GVWR.

Class C — Any single vehicle, or combination of vehicles, that does not meet the definition of Class A or Class B, but is either designed to transport 16 or more passengers, including the driver, or is placarded for hazardous materials.

Knowledge and Skills Tests: States develop their own tests which must be at least as stringent as the Federal standards. The FMCSA has prepared model driver and examiner manuals and tests and distributed them to the states to use, if they wish.

- The general knowledge test must contain at least 30 questions.
- To pass the knowledge tests (general and endorsement), applicants must correctly answer at least 80 percent of the questions.

- To pass the skills test, applicants must successfully perform all the required skills (listed in 49 CFR 383.113). The skills test must be taken in a vehicle representative of the type of vehicle that the applicant operates or expects to operate.

Other States, employers, training facilities, governmental departments and agencies, and private institutions can serve as *third party skills testers* for the State under the following criteria:

- Tests must be the same as those given by the State.
- Examiners must meet the same qualifications as State examiners.

- States must conduct an on-site inspection at least once a year.
  At least annually, State employees must evaluate the programs by taking third party tests as if they were test applicants, or by testing a sample of drivers tested by the third party and then comparing pass/fail rates.
- The State's agreement with the third party skills tester must allow the FHWA and the State to conduct random examinations, inspections, and audits without prior notice.

The states determine the license fee, the renewal cycle, most renewal procedures, and continue to decide the age, medical and other driver qualifications of their intrastate commercial drivers. Interstate drivers must meet the longstanding Federal driver qualifications (49 CFR 391).

All CLD's must contain the following information:

- The words "Commercial Driver's Li- cense" or "CDL."
- The driver's full name, signature, and address.
- The driver's date of birth, sex and height.
- Color photograph or digitalized image of the driver.

- The driver's state license number.
- The name of the issuing state.
- The date of issuance and the date of the expiration of the license.
- The class of vehicle that the driver is authorized to operate.
- Notation of the "air brake" restriction, if issued.
- The endorsement's for which the driver has qualified.

States may issue learner's permits for behind-the-wheel training on public highways as long as learner's permit holders are required to be accompanied by someone with a valid CDL appropriate for that vehicle and the learner's permits are issued for limited time periods.

CDL holders are subject to the following penalties, disqualifications and standards. Violations may result in civil or criminal penalties and the loss of the CDL.

Penalties: The Federal penalty to a driver who violates the CDL requirements is a civil penalty of up to $2,500 or, in aggravated cases, criminal penalties of up to $5,000 in fines and/or up to 90 days in prison. An employer is also subject to a penalty of up to $10,000, if (s)he knowingly uses a driver to operate a CMV without a valid CDL.

Drivers must be disqualified and lose their privilege to drive for one year for driving under the influence of a controlled substance or alcohol, or leaving the scene of an accident, or using a CMV to commit a felony.

Drivers must be disqualified and lose their privilege to drive for three years for committing any of the one- year offenses while operating a CMV that is placarded for hazardous materials.

Drivers must be disqualified and for committing a second offense of any of the one-year or three-year offenses, or using a CMV to commit a felony involving manufacturing, distributing, or dispensing controlled substances.

However, states have the option to reduce certain lifetime disqualifications to a minimum disqualification of ten years if the driver completes a driver rehabilitation program approved by the state.

If a CDL holder is disqualified from operating a CMV, the state may issue this person a license to operate non-commercial vehicles. However, states cannot issue a "conditional" or "hardship" CDL or any other type of limited driving privileges to continue driving a CMV to a disqualified driver.

Convictions for out-of-state violations are treated the same as convictions for violations that are committed in the driver's home state. The Commercial Driver's License Information System (CDLIS), to which states must be connected, ensures that convictions a driver receives outside his/her home state are transmitted to the home state so that the disqualifications can be applied.

BAC Standards: The FHWA has established **0.04 percent** as the blood alcohol concentration (BAC) level at or above which a CMV driver is considered to be driving under the influence of alcohol and subject to the disqualification sanctions in the Act.

Employer Notifications: A driver must notify his/her employer within thirty days of a conviction for any traffic violation, except parking, regardless of the nature of the violation or the type of vehicle driven at the time. An Owner- Operator under a lease contract is considered to be an employee of the carrier and must therefore report violations to the carrier.

The employer must be notified if a driver's license is suspended, revoked, canceled, or if (s)he is disqualified from driving. The notification must be made by the end of the next business day following receipt of the suspension, revocation, cancellation, lost privilege or disqualification. from driving. Violations of this requirement may result in civil or criminal penalties. Source: www.fmcsa.gov.

CDL Manuals and Knowledge Tests may be obtained from the Motor Vehicle Division of the driver's home state. The address and telephone numbers are listed in the blue pages under State Government in the telephone directories. Most states also provide CDL information on-line.

Most jurisdictions offer their CDL manuals in English only. However, the following jurisdictions offer the CDL manual in Spanish in some form: Arizona, California, Idaho, Michigan, Minnesota, New Jersey, New York, Texas, and D.C.

The following seventeen jurisdictions provide the CDL Knowledge Test in Spanish in some form: Arizona, California, Colorado, Delaware, Florida, Georgia, Idaho, Iowa, Minnesota, New Jersey, New York, Oregon, Texas,
Virginia, Washington, Wisconsin, and D.C.

Average time to complete the skills tests is 31 minutes for pre-trip inspections, 22 minutes for the basic control skills, and 40 minutes for the on- road driving. Source: AAMVA 1997 Commercial Driver's License Survey.

Under the PATRIOT Act of 2001, applicants for CDL's with a hazardous materials endorsement and drivers who already have a CDL with a hazmat endorsement are required to clear an FBI background check, must be finger- printed, and the endorsements must be renewed at least every five years.

Enforcement of this rule was to begin November 3, 2003, but states have asked that enforcement of this rule be postponed because all the systems needed are not yet in place. Fingerprinting is now scheduled to begin January 31, 2005.

Eventually, all truckers may be required to undergo background checks with fingerprints or some other biometric identifier. Furthermore, the Department of Homeland Security is working on a program to create a Transportation Worker Identification Credential, which is a type of universal security card which could also serve as CDL for truck drivers.

CSA 2010

The purpose of the CSA 2010 initiative is to develop more effective andefficient methods for FMCSA, together with industry and state partners, to achieve its mission of reducing commercial motor vehicle (CMV) crashes, fatalities, and injuries.

How will your operation be impacted by CSA2010? Because CSA2010 will audit ALL carriers and drivers and their violations, andwill impose harsher fines and penalties than ever before, it will be imperative that your company understands the changes this new initiative brings to the trucking industry. CSA2010 will employ COMPASS, an electronic database for keeping records on carrier safety ratings. This system, in addition to data gathered from roadsideviolations, and crash reports, will enable the FMCSA to monitor carrier performance, and identify those requiring intervention.

Under CSA2010, Interventions can begin and end with a Warning Letter, or can be broadened to include off-site investigations (records audits), and finally on-site investigations. All of these can include development of corrective action plans, but may also involve fines!

Because **CSA2010 will audit ALL carriers and drivers, identifies over 1000 possible violations, and will impose harsher fines and penalties than ever before**, it is imperative that your company understands the changes this new initiative brings to the trucking industry!

Unfortunately, many companies who are "satisfactory" under the currentSafe Stat system WILL be found non compliant and placed in INTERVENTION status with the DOT under CSA2010. If you find yourself in this unenviable situation,you will be required to develop a measureable, results-oriented safety-training plan in order to respond to and remove yourself from intervention status. You need responsive reporting and must demonstrate to the DOT that your employees and drivers are not only going thru the safety training necessary to respond to the issues which resulted in intervention, but you should also have 3rd Party documented test results, with which to demonstrate their progress!

The CSA 2010 Operational Model has three major components:

> Measurement - CSA 2010 measures safety performance in new ways, using inspection and crash results to identify carriers whose behaviors could reasonably lead to crashes.
>
> Evaluation - CSA 2010 helps FMCSA and its State Partners to correct high risk behavior by contacting more carriers and drivers, with interventions tailored to their specific safety problem, as well as a new safety fitness determination methodology.
>
> Intervention - CSA 2010 covers the full spectrum of safety issues – from how data is collected, evaluated, and shared to how enforcement officials can intervene most effectively and efficiently to improve safety on our roads.

Safety Measurement System

Within the Comprehensive Safety Analysis (CSA 2010) Operational Model, the Safety Measurement System (SMS) quantifies the on-road safety performance of carriers and drivers to identify candidates for interventions, to determine the specific safety problems exhibited by a carrier or driver, and to monitor whether safety problems are improving or worsening. SMS replaces Safe Stat in the new Operational Model. The carrier SMS uses a motor carrier's data from roadside inspections, including all safety-based violations, State- reported crashes, and the Federal motor carrier census to quantify performance in the following Behavior Analysis Safety Improvement Categories (BASICs).

CSA 2010 BASICs:

Unsafe Driving — Operation of commercial motor vehicles (CMVs) by drivers in a dangerous or careless manner. *Example Violations:* Speeding, reckless driving, improper lane change, and inattention.
(FMCSR Parts 392 and 397)

Fatigued Driving (Hours-of-Service) — Operation of CMVs by drivers who are ill, fatigued, or in non-compliance with the Hours-of-Service (HOS) regulations. This BASIC includes violations of regulations pertaining to logbooks as they relate to HOS requirements and the management of CMV driver fatigue. *Example Violations:* HOS, logbook, and operating a CMV while ill or fatigued. (FMCSR Parts 392 and 395)

Driver Fitness — Operation of CMVs by drivers who are unfit to operate a CMV due to lack of training, experience, or medical qualifications. *Example Violations:* Failure to have a valid and appropriate commercial driver's license and being medically un- qualified to operate a CMV. (FMCSR Parts 383 and 391)

Controlled Substances/Alcohol — Operation of CMVs by drivers who are impaired due to alcohol, illegal drugs, and misuse of prescription or over- the-counter medications. *Example Violations:* Use or possession of con- trolled substances/alcohol. (FMCSR Parts 382 and 392)

Vehicle Maintenance — Failure to properly maintain a CMV. *Example Violations:* Brakes, lights, and other mechanical defects, and failure to make required repairs. (FMCSR Parts 393 and 396)

Cargo-Related — Failure to properly prevent shifting loads, spilled or dropped cargo, overloading, and unsafe handling of hazardous materials on a CMV. *Example Violations:* Improper load securement, cargo retention, and hazardous material handling. (FMCSR Parts 392, 393, 397 and HM Violations)

Crash Indicator — Histories or patterns of high crash involvement, including frequency and severity. It is based on information from State reported crashes.

A carrier's measurement for each BASIC depends on:
The number of adverse safety events (violations related to that BASIC or crashes)
The severity of violations or crashes
When the adverse safety events occurred (more recent events are weighted more heavily).

After a measurement is determined, the carrier is then placed in a peer group (e.g., other carriers with similar numbers of inspections). Percentiles from 0 to 100 are then determined by comparing the BASIC measurements of the carrier to the measurements of other carriers in the peer group. 100 indicates the worst performance.

Safety Evaluation

Safety evaluation is the process of determining how to address carriers with poor safety performance.

The Safety Measurement System (SMS) allows FMCSA to more effectively evaluate safety performance using new measures for identifying which carriers require what type of intervention using a policy-driven process called intervention selection, and

determining which carriers should be proposed "Unfit" to operate, using a regulatory process called Safety Fitness Determination (SFD).

(An *Unfit Suspension* will prohibit a carrier from

operating, based on the conclusion of a SFD. The details of Unfit Suspension will be described in the SFD Rulemaking.)

FMCSA is developing a SFD methodology, subject to ongoing rulemaking, to re- place the current system that is solely dependent on the onsite compliance review results. The SFD will expand the use of on-road performance as calculated in the SMS and include results of all investigations. It will also allow FMCSA to determine safety fitness on a larger segment of the industry.

Intervention

FMCSA and State partners will use measurement results to identify carriers for CSA 2010 interventions. These interventions will offer an expanded suite of tools ranging from warning letters to comprehensive on site investigations. These tools supplement the labor-intensive compliance review (CR) to better address the specific safety problems identified.

CSA 2010 investigators will be equipped to systematically evaluate why safety problems are occurring, to recommend remedies, to encourage corrective action(s), and, where corrective action is inadequate, to invoke strong penalties. Interventions will provide carriers with the information necessary to understand their safety problems and to change unsafe behavior early on. Interventions under CSA 2010 can be broken into 3 basic categories, which are described in detail below: early contact, investigation, and follow-on.

Early Contact

Warning Letter - Correspondence sent to a carrier's place of business that specifically identifies a deficient BASIC(s) and outlines possible consequences of continued safety problems. The warning letter provides instructions for accessing carrier safety data and measurement as well as a point of contact.

Carrier Access to Safety Data and Measurement - Carriers have access to their measurement results (BASICs scores), as well as the inspection reports and violations that went into those results. With this information, carriers can chart a course of self-improvement. Carriers can also monitor this data for accuracy and challenge it as necessary through FMCSA's Data Qs system: https://dataqs.fmcsa.dot.gov/login.asp.

Targeted Roadside Inspection - CSA 2010 provides roadside inspectors with data that identifies a carrier's specific safety problems, by BASIC, based on the new measurement system. Targeted roadside inspections occur at permanent and temporary roadside inspection locations where connectivity to the SMS information is available. As Commercial Vehicle Information Systems and Networks (CVISN) technologies evolve they will be incorporated into the roadside inspections.

Investigation

Offsite Investigation - A carrier is required to submit documents to FMCSA ora State Partner. These documents are used to evaluate the safety

problems identified through the SMS and to determine their root causes. Types of documents requested may include third party documents such as toll receipts, border crossing records, or drug testing records. The goal is to identify issues responsible for poor safety performance. If the carrier does not submit requested documents they may be subject to an onsite investigation or to subpoena records (see below).

Onsite Investigation - Focused - The purpose of this intervention is to evaluate the safety problems identified through the SMS and their root causes. An onsite focused investigation may be selected when deficiencies in two or less BASICs exist. Onsite "focused" investigations target specific problem areas (for example, maintenance records), while onsite "comprehensive" investigations address all asects of the carrier's operation.

Onsite Investigation - Comprehensive - This intervention is similar to a CR andtakes place at the carrier's place of business. It is used when the carrier exhibits broad and complex safety problems through continually deficient BASICs, worsening multiple BASICs (three or more), or a fatal crash or complaint.

Follow-on

Cooperative Safety Plan (CSP) - Implemented by the carrier, this safety improvement plan is voluntary. The carrier and FMCSA collaboratively create a plan, based on a standard template, to address the underlying problems resulting from the car- rier's substandard safety performance.

Notice of Violation (NOV) - The NOV is a formal notice of safety deficiencies that requires a response from the carrier. It is used when the regulatory violations discovered are severe enough to warrant formal action but not a civil penalty (fine). It is also used in cases where the violation is immediately correctable and the level of, or desire for, cooperation is high. To avoid further intervention, including fines, the carrier must provide evidence of corrective action or initiate a successful challenge to the violation.

Notice of Claim (NOC) - A NOC is issued in cases where the regulatoryviolations are severe enough to warrant assessment and issuance of civil penalties.

Operations Out-of-Service Order (OOS) - An order requiring the carrier to cease all motor vehicle operations.

Choosing A Legal Business Structure

Sole proprietorships, partner- ships, corporations, and limited liability companies are the most common legal structures for small businesses. No one legal structure is right for all small businesses. Whether starting the business as a sole proprietor or choosing one of the more complicated organizational structures depends on several factors.

A **sole proprietorship** is the basic and simple form of a business
organization and has no existence apart from the owner. The spouse can be an informal owner of your sole proprietor- ship.
The business liabilities are also the owner's liabilities. Ownership (proprietary) interest ends when the owner dies.
The owner undertakes the risks of business to the extent of all of his/ her assets. There is no differentiation between the business and the owner's private assets. The owner is responsible for loss, gain or damage.
The owner is responsible for estimated tax payments on a quarterly basis to the IRS, if the estimated tax payment is more than $500. Sole proprietors pay taxes on business income on their personal tax return.

A **partnership** is the relationship existing between two or more persons who join together to carry on a trade or business. A business with more than one person that is not incorporated or organized as an LLC is a partnership by default.

The term partnership includes a syndicate, group, pool, joint venture, or other unincorporated organizations that carries on a business and is not classified as a trust, estate or corporation.

Each person joining the partner- ship contributes money, property, labor or skill and expects to share in the profits and losses of the business.

A partnership agreement or added modifications may be oral or written. If there is an oral agreement, witnesses should be present or it should be recorded on tape.

Generally, a partner's share of income, gain, loss, deductions, or credits is determined by the partnership agreement. The liabilities of a partnership are determined by the number of shares (s)he acquires when signing the agreement.

However, the liability is every partner's responsibility including his personal assets pending on the percentage (s)he owns in a partnership.

A partnership is not a taxable entity, and each partner is responsible for paying estimated taxes and filing tax returns.

A **corporation** is the most important form to organize a business be- cause it comes into existence by an act of the state and therefore is a legal entity. It has a definite existence through legal papers filed with the State, generally the Secretary of State or the Corporation Commission.

A corporation has perpetual existence as long as it is compliant with annual filing requirements of the Secretary of State or the Corporation Commission.

Registration of a corporate name shall contain the word "corporation," "company," or "incorporated," or shall contain an abbreviation of one of such words.

The corporate name should not be the same as, or deceptively similar to, the name of any domestic corporation existing under the law of the same state in which the new corporation will be registered.

A corporation provides protection from personal liability for business debts. The liability of its owners is limited to their investments, and their personal estates are not liable for the obligations of the corporation. However, failure to comply with and follow corporate formalities or keep adequate records can result in the loss of the limited liability status.

Corporations consist of shareholders, who are the owners of the business. A minimum of two persons is required to create a corporation. A board of directors, which is elected by the shareholders, manages the business.

S Corporations: Certain corporations can choose to qualify under Sub-chapter S of the Internal Revenue Code to avoid the imposition of income taxes at the corporate level while retaining all the advantages of a corporation. Income from an S Corporation is taxed as personal income on Schedule E (Form 1040).

A corporation must meet these requirements to qualify

for a S Corporation status:

- Be a domestic corporation.
- Not be a member of an affiliated group of corporations.
- Have only one class of stock. Not all shareholders need to have the same voting rights.

- Have 35 or fewer shareholders.
- No shareholder of the corporation can be a non-resident alien.
- Shareholders must be individuals, estates or certain trusts.
- Corporations, partnerships and non qualifying trusts cannot be shareholders.

Limited Liabilities Companies (LLC) combine some of the best attributes of corporations and partnerships, including limited personal liability and one level of taxation. LLC owners report business income and losses on their personal in- come tax returns, thus avoiding double taxation.

Articles of organization must include the name of the LLC, the address of the registered office, the name of a statutory agent, a dissolution date, and information about management.

Filing requirements and fees are similar to those of a corporation.

- **Each form of business has advantages and disadvantages. The independent truck-owner operator should carefully study the options and make a decision based on his or her personal circumstances and applicable state and tax laws.**
- **Once the owner-operator has selected a form of business organization, (s)he must make sure that (s)he understands the specifics of that structure and follows the requirements to stay compliant with federal, state, local and tax laws.**

Buying Your Truck

Starting a business requires a significant capital investment. And few start-ups have succeeded on a shoe-string budget. This is especially true for the capital-intensive transportation industry. The start-up Owner-Operator needs cash for the down payment on a truck, the registration, permits, and insurance as well as for the day-to-day operation of the truck until revenue starts flowing in.

Buying that first truck is an emotional experience, and the decision will have long-term implications. Therefore, you must carefully research the marketand choose well maintained, easy-to-handle and reliable equipment.

Before selecting a truck, the Owner-Operator needs to establish business connections where (s)he can get loads. That means talking directly to manufacturers and businesses, transportation brokers, and/or obtaining information from carriers about their lease-on programs, and checking references. Owner Operators can also utilize a consulting service that will help and teach Owner Operator's how to establish business relationships and how to find good paying loads. TruckingSuccess.com offers such a consulting service for a modest fee. To sign up for this service, please call (602) 864-8056

Although you may dream of a fancy, shiny new truck, a good quality used truck with a modest monthly payment will make more sense for the Owner-Operator who has to gain industry experience. Most Owner- Operators prefer long-nose trucks, but for the beginner cab-overs offer better value for the money, because they are considerably cheaper than conventional trucks.

A buyer can choose from a huge selection of pre-owned trucks, which are offered through Internet auctions, used truck sale magazines, dealerships, private parties, and manufacturers. For a listing of the largest used truck locater, visit www.putrucks.com.

Also consider such factors as fuel efficiency and cab comfort because you spend most of your day driving. Fuel costs make up a significant part of the operating expenses, and a fuel efficient truck can greatly improve the business's bottom line.

An Owner-Operator will need between $5,000 to $10,000 just for the cost associated with the purchaseof a good used truck in addition to financing the rest of the truck's purchase price.

Used truck prices range from: $10,000 to over $50,000, but a good four to five-year-old Cab-over should sell for approximately $20,000, with a down payment of $4,000 to $5,000. The finance company will require a down payment of 10 to 20 percent, depending on the buyer's credit rating, and may also require a cosigner. Interest rates generally are higher than regular vehicle loans because only a few companies specialize in truck financing.

Additional expenditures include the registration fee, license plate and operating permits, as well as insurance premiums. The Owner-Operator will need several types of coverage. Department of Transportation regulations require liability coverage, however, other coverage, such as physical damage or workers' compensation, may be necessary to comply with state regulations or to meet shipper requirements. Insurance rates have significantly in- creased due to losses associated with the terrorist attacks. Most Owner- Operators make a down-payment and finance the annual premium, making monthly payments. About 15 insurance companies specialize in truck insurance, and most require three monthly premiums upfront, which amounts to several thousand dollars, and nine monthly payments.

The Owner-Operator will need financial resources to cover several weeks of operating expenses until revenue starts flowing in.

Some brokers may pay right away when you present documents that you have delivered the load, but most brokers and lease-on carriers will make weekly or biweekly disbursements.

Additionally, you will incur smaller expenditures for a CB radio, having your business name and DOT number painted on your truck, buying a ELD and office supplies, as well as supplies and items you will need for the sleeper.

Selecting a good used truck

A lot of equipment is available on the used truck market, but as the industry continues to struggle with high fuel costs, it is important to select aerodynamic and fuel-efficient equipment to reduce operating costs.

The Used Truck Association (UTA) has released a set of guidelines for "industry standard" trade terms and conditions. These are used to establish the condition of a used truck, asagreed by the buyer and seller.

The UTA Trade Terms & Conditions covers engines, drive-trains, brakes, tires, frames, cabs, sleepers, and bodies. It also takes into consideration de- identification, safety inspections and fleet trades. A free copy is available at www.uta.org. Source: Transportation Equipment News.

Visit the truck dealerships in your area and check the equipment they have in stock. You will hopefully find several trucks that meet your specifications. When you talk to a salesperson, ask questions and take notes. You should have prepared a list of items you need to know to help you make a purchase decision. Some of the questions you need to ask should include:

- How many miles are on the chassis?
- How many miles are on the major components such as the engine, transmission, differentials, turbo charger, power steering, and air conditioning system?
- Is the truck or certain components still under factory/manufacturer warranty?
- Does the dealership offer a warranty?
- Are used equipment warranties available for you to purchase?

Who performed the truck **maintenance and where?**
- Are maintenance records available?
- For what type of service was the truck used for?
- How many previous owners?
- In what climate was the truck operated?
- Does the truck have all original components?
- If not, which components have been replaced and why?
- Has the engine been overhauled?
- Has the truck been in an accident or collision?

Ask additional questions and demand explanations or clarifications if you do not understand what the sales person tells you.

You need to make sure that you learn as much as possible about the truck that you want to purchase, and an honest dealer will respect that. Also resist any pressure to close the deal until you have all the answers and explanations you need to make your final decision. Keep in mind that you invest a great deal of money in this truck and your success as an Owner-Operator will in part depend on your ability to select a well- maintained used truck whose major components will perform well for you.

Also perform a close and careful visual inspection. Start by walking around the vehicle, looking for physical damage such as body work, bent wheels, broken springs, frayed air lines, chipped or cracked lines, metal fatigue, welding marks, and anything unusual.

Then check the engine. Tilt the cab or hood and check the outer surface for leaks. Also look for signs of leakage on the side of the engine block just below the cylinder head. Ask for an explanation if it appears as if the engine was steam cleaned.

Next, pull out the oil dipstick and check for water beads. If you find water on the dipstick, it may indicate a sealing problem. Again, ask for an explanation. Then start the engine and let it idle for about fifteen minutes and check for leaks again. Ask for a test drive and take the salesperson with you to answer any questions you may have. The test drive may reveal trouble spots or problems that would otherwise hide by only idling the engine. While you drive the truck, also check for smoke. Heavy black smoke may indicate injector, pump or engine breathing problems. The next major component to check is the transmission. If the truck has a transmission temperature gauge, watch it. The normal transmission temperature should be 200 degrees Fahrenheit or below. You should also check the transmission and rear axles for leaks. Then carefully check for cracks on the frame and make sure no welding was done at the frame rails.

Congratulations if you found the perfect truck with which to begin your trucking business. If not, do not hesitate to walk away from a bad deal and start searching again.

Maintenance and Repair

Getting your truck serviced regularly and keeping it well maintained will help prevent costly repairs and breakdowns on the road as well as extends the lifespan of your equipment.

Your truck dealership will perform some of the service work, if your truck is covered by a manufacturer's warranty or if you purchased a used truck warranty. However, dealerships usually charge higher prices than independently owned shops.

Many service stations at truck stops offer specials for basic services. You may find it more convenient and time efficient to get routine maintenance such as oil changes done at truck stops while you are on the road.

As an alternative, find a small and independently owned repair shop where you can develop a personal relationship with the owner and mechanics. This will help you get your truck repaired or serviced without long waiting periods, maybe even on weekends, so you can get back on the road without delay. This will reduce unproductive downtime.

Regular preventive maintenance and inspections will help you spot minor problems early and you can repair them before they turn into major problems. The truck is your business and you have to keep it in excellent operating condition in order to run a safe and profitable business.

Make the daily pre-trip inspection part of your preventive maintenance routine. During the daily inspection, check a list of items on the truck and trailer's in– and outside. Follow the same daily routine, so nothing gets missed or overlooked. If you are leased to a carrier, you may be required to follow a specific inspection pattern. Otherwise, use this outline:

- Overview of the entire tractor-trailer:
- Engine compartment check fluid levels, fluid leaks, belts, battery, wiring, and compressor.
- Inside the cab start the engine, check gauges and controls, check the windshield and function of wipers and washer, windows and mirrors, emergency equipment, test air brake, check steering, the log book.
- Check lights high and low beams, four-way flashers.
- Walk around, check tires, wheels, turn signals, couplings, fifth wheel, landing gear, brakes, axles, sliders, spare tire, fuel

tanks, exhaust system, cargo-securement, suspension.
- Perform brake check.
- Check signal lights.

Federal law requires a driver to complete an inspection report after each day. Any defects noted must be repaired. The mechanic performing the repairs must sign the report andcertify that repairs have been made. The inspection report serves as a reminder of items to check after eachday of driving. It also provides proof of inspection and the repairs.

The Department of Transportation (DOT) also conducts roadside inspections, and officers can legally stop a truck at any time. This officer may be a federal or state department of transportation (DOT) employee, a highway patrol officer, weigh master, or other government official.

This inspection can take place along a roadside, at a rest area, a scale, or at a port of entry station. If your truck fails the inspection, the officer can declare the truck "out of service." This means you cannot drive your vehicle until the repairs are made and a re-inspection takes place. An inspection takes about thirty minutes. When your truck passes the inspection, you will receive a sticker that is valid for three months.

A preventive maintenance program consists of the above outlined daily routine check and the regular service check. These service checks include replacing parts before they wear out or fail.

Service checks have three levels. Items covered at the basic service Level A include grease jobs, brake adjustments, check of fluid levels, tread depth of tires, and leaks. Level B includes all the work done for Level A plus changing the oil and the oil and fuel filter. Level C service includes engine tuning, brake jobs, and replacing or rebuilding worn and failing parts.
Climatic or seasonal weather conditions require specific preventive maintenance. When you operate in hot weather

conditions such as in the South- western U.S., you need to check the condition of coolant hoses and the and the tightness of the water pump and fan belts regularly. In cold weather conditions, regularly check the antifreeze level, and the heaters and defrosters.

Operating Authority

The **Federal Highway Administration (FHA)** and its agencies is the regulatory authority for the trucking industry. A motor carrier must obtain an interstate operating authority from FHA before the carrier can engage in interstate trucking.

The truly independent trucker prefers to have his/her own operating authority; however, the start-up Owner- Operator may choose to use another carrier's authority by leasing on to that carrier.

If you are a relatively inexperienced Owner-Operator, leasing on will allow you to get hands-on industry experience and a regular paycheck while the carrier handles the details of pro- viding the operating permits, loads, a trailer, fuel cards, etc.

Carrier leases are governed by federal laws. You can locate the applicable statutes in Title 49 of the United States Code, 49 CFR Part 376, Lease and Interchange of Vehicles. Onlinesearch for "49CR376" at www.access.gpo.gov/nara/cfr.index.html. And recently a U.S. appeals court has ruledthat Owner-Operators have the right to sue carriers that do not comply with federal leasing regulations. Many trucking companies now offer lease programs for owner operators as well as lease-purchase programs. Most programs sound very good, but please be aware of unscrupulous carriers. They can cost you thousands of dollars and put you out of business.

If you consider leasing on, obtain copies of leases from several carriers that interest you and study them carefully. If a carrier does not want to provide you with a copy for your review, pass on it. Truth-in-leasing laws entitle you to a copy of the lease before you sign it. Make sure you understand the implications before you sign a lease, and never pick up a load before you read the lease.

Provisions a lease should contain and specify:

- It must clearly detail the responsibility of the carrier and the owner- operator with respect to cost such as fuel, fuel taxes, deadheading, tolls and permits, base plates and licenses, and what happens to any unused portions of these items.
- It must clearly specify who is responsible for loading and unloading, and who pays for lumping.
- The carrier must pay you for loads within 15 days of submission of the paperwork.
- If you get paid on a percentage basis, you are entitled to a copy of a rated freight bill before or when you get paid for the load.
- Only items specified in the lease can be deducted from the settlement.
- The lease must state the amount of the escrow fund and to which items it may be applied. The carrier must pro- vide an accounting of the escrow fund, either on the settlement form or once a month on a separate form. The lease must give the owner-operator the right to ask for an account of the fund on demand. And while the carrier controls the fund, it must pay interest. All deductions from the escrow fund must be specified in the lease, and a final account of the fund must be pro- vided and the balance be paid no later than 45 days from the owner operator's last day with the carrier.

- Terminate your lease in writing and within any specified termination period.

The carrier and you must sign an original and two copies of the lease. The carrier keeps the original and you must keep one copy in your truck. File the other copy with your business documents.

Never sign a lease under pressure and in haste. Question everything you do not understand, because once your signature is on that document, it is a legally binding contract. Avoid leases for specific periods of time such as three months or a year. Instead, opt for a month- to-month lease so you can give notice and terminate your lease within a reasonable time should things not work out. Always pay for your own base plate and fuel tax, because many carriers charge a flat rate and fail to give an accounting and refund of over- payments. Avoid unknown carriers and check an incorporated carrier's status with the Corporation Commission.

If the information on file with Corporation Commission is scant, avoid the carrier. Ask for references and talk to other Owner-Operators that are leased on to the company with which you are negotiating. If you get negative feedback, reconsider your choice. And always ask to see the equipment you're signing on to. Don't sign anything before you can inspect what you're getting.

The once complicated process of obtaining your own interstate operating authority has been simplified and you can even apply on line.

Why should you get your own authority? The answer is simple: it will give you more independence to make decisionshow to run your operation. You can find your own loads and negotiate the freight rates, or you can work with reputable brokers to find loads for you.

You will need to follow these steps to get your authority:

- Obtain an **application** for Motor Property Carrier & Broker Authority from the Federal Motor Carrier Safety Administration

(FMCSA), either by mail or online at http://diy.dot.gov. The website also includes information about filing requirements.

- Obtain **liability insurance**. Federal regulations require all for-hire carriers to have liability insurance. The minimum coverage is $750,000, if you do not haul hazardous materials. Hazmat carriers must have $1 million to $5 million minimum coverage, depending on what they haul. In addition, common carriers need a minimum of $100,000 in cargo insurance. Your insurance company or agent must send the needed forms to FMCSA. They must be submitted within 90 days of application.

- You need a **legal process agent** for each state in which you operate. If there are legal proceedings against you, the legal process agent is the person who will officially receive any papers served. Your insurance company may provide this service to you. If not, companies that offer compliance services are also legal process agents.

- Obtain **DOT number** by submitting a Motor Carrier Identification Report (Form MCS-150) and obtain a DOT number from FMCSA. You must do this before you begin operations, and your DOT number along with your company name must appear on your vehicle(s).

The UCR (Unified Carrier Registration) is a program that replaced the (SSRS) Single State Registration System. The UCR Program requires individuals and companies that operate commercial motor vehicles in interstate or international commerce to register their business with a participating state and pay an annual fee based on the size of their fleet. This includes ALL carriers and truck owners, private, exempt, or for hire. Kentucky, New Mexico, New York, and Oregon still require additional tax credentials.

- Obtain **IFTA license** from your base state. (Please see Registration section for details about UCR, IRP and IFTA.)

Keeping Business Records

When you start your own trucking business, you are also responsible for keeping accurate records, making tax payments and filing tax returns.

Except in a few cases, the law does not require any special kind of records. You may choose any system that is best suited for your business and that clearly shows your income. An accountant can help you decide which system to use. If you do not have an accountant yet, hire a trustworthy accountant who has knowledge of the trucking industry.

The accountant can help you set up a record and bookkeeping system., and will also prepare your tax returns. However, you can save money by doing most of the bookkeeping tasks yourself. If you use a computer in your business, a basic bookkeeping program can assist you in this task. If you have no bookkeeping experience, your accountant or a bookkeeping service can keep your books for you, but it will cost you money. Your accountant can also prepare monthly, quarterly, and year-end financial statements, so you can measure the progress of your business. You should also keep personal and business finances separate. Therefore, you should open a business checking account.

Reasons to Keep Records:
- Business owners must keep records.
- Good records help monitor the progress of your business and help you determine what changes you must make. Good records increase the likelihood of your success.
- Good records help prepare accurate financial statements, which include income (profit and loss) statements and balance sheets. These statements can help you in dealing with your bank or creditors.
- Good records identify the source of receipts. You receive

money or property from various sources and need to identify and separate business and non-business receipts and taxable and non-taxable income.
- Good records help you keep track of deductible expense.
- Good records help in the preparation of your tax return.

You must keep your business re- cords available at all times for inspection by the Internal Revenue Service (IRS). If the IRS conducts an audit and examines any of your tax returns, you may be asked to explain the items re- ported. A complete set of records will speed up the examination and may avoid additional taxation.

Kinds of Records to Keep:
- The law does not require any special kind of records. You may choose any system suited to yourbusiness that clearly shows your income.
- The business you are in affects the type of records you need to keep for federal and state tax purposes. You should set up your books using an accounting system that clearly shows your income for your tax year.
- The books must show your gross income as well as your deductions and credits. In addition, you must keep supporting documents. Purchases, sales, payroll, and other transactions you have in your business will generate supporting documents such as invoices and receipts.
- These documents contain the information you need to record in your books. It is important to keep these documents in an orderly fashion and in a safe place.

How Long to Keep Records:

- You must keep your records for as long as they may be needed for the administration of any provision of the Internal Revenue Code. Generally, this means you must keep records that support an item of income or deduction on a return until the period of limitations for that re- turn runs out.
- The period of limitations is the period of time in which you can amend your return to claim a credit or refund. It is

three years after the date your return is due or filed and two years after the date the tax is paid. The IRS has three years from the date you file your return to assess any additional tax. If someone files a fraudulent return or no returns at all, the IRS has a much longer period of time to assess additional taxes.

If you have employees, you must keep all employment tax records for at least four years after the date the tax becomes due or is paid, whichever is later.

Accounting Periods: Every tax payer, business or individual, must figure taxable income and file a tax re- turn on the basis of an annual accounting period.

Your "tax year" is the annual accounting period you use for keeping your records and reporting of your income and expenses. The accounting periods you can use are **(1) a calendar year or (2) a fiscal year.** If your tax year begins on January 1 and ends on December 31, the due date for filing your tax return is April 15, following the tax year. The due date for corporate tax returns is March 15, following the tax year.

A fiscal tax year consists of twelve consecutive months ending on the last day of any month except December. The due date for filing your tax return is 2.5 months after your fiscal year ended. For example, the fiscal year runs from July 1 to June 30, you file your tax return on or before September 15.

Accounting Methods: Generally, you may use any of the following methods:

- ☐ Cash method,
- ☐ Accrual method,
  Special methods of accounting for certain items of income and expenses, and
- ☐ Combination (hybrid) method using elements of two or more of the above.

Most individuals and many small businesses with no inventories use the **Cash Method** of accounting. This method cannot be used by (1) corporations (other than S corp.), (2) partner ships having a corporation (other than an S corp.) as a partner, and (3) tax shelters. With this method, you include in your gross income all items of income you actually or constructively receive during the year and you must deduct expenses in the tax year in which you actually pay them.

Under an **Accrual Method** of ac- counting, income generally is reported in the year earned, and expenses are deducted or capitalized in the year incurred. The purpose of this accounting method is to match your income and expenses in the correct year.

Special Methods of accounting are used for certain items of income or expenses such as depreciation, amortization and depletion, deduction for bad debts, and installment sales.

Combination method: Generally, you may use any combination of cash, accrual, and special methods of accounting if the combination clearly shows income and you use it consistently. However, restrictions apply.

Change in Accounting Method. When you first file your return, you may choose any permitted accounting method. However, the method you choose must be used consistently from year to year and clearly show your income. If you want to change your ac- counting method after your first return is filed, you must first get consent from the IRS.

Please note: *The information presented in this section is of a general and informative nature and does not constitute tax or legal advice.*

Setting Up Your Own Record Keeping System. In order to comply with the requirements for keeping accurate records as discussed above, you need to device your own record keeping system. Most of your financial transactions will be in cash, check or credit cards and will take place while you are out on the road conducting your business. To keep track of your expenses on the road, always obtain a receipt when you buy something or pay for service. Carry a receipt book with you to record payment of lumper fees, etc. Make sure all receipts are dated, show a (business) name, and the purpose of the purchase or payment.

Use your business checks to pay for expenses such as truck payments, repairs, supplies, insurance premium payments, and license or permit fees. Match the canceled checks with the corresponding invoices or bills and you will have an accurate receipt.

When you travel, keep all your receipts in a trip envelope. Then collect all your receipts, invoices and canceled checks from your trip envelopes and file them in a separate file in chronological order. When you do your monthly bookkeeping, all you have to do is separate them by type of expenses.

You also must keep track of your Accounts Payable, that is money owed to you. When you receive a payment, attach the check stub to the corresponding invoice and file it until you do your monthly bookkeeping.

Accurate records will reflect the financial state of your business and tell you if you are making or losing money. You can also make comparisons from month to month or year to year, to determine if your business is growing and remains stagnant. Additionally, accurate records will help ensure the tax assessment on you income is fair.

The following documents can assist you to keep accurate records, organize your business, save you money, and make your business profitable:

- **Trip report** — recaps your travel routes and how many miles you have driven.
- **Expense report** — summarizes your trip expenses for meals, motels, showers, tolls, fuel, etc.

- **Bank statements** — shows the activity of your business bank account.
- **Settlement sheet** — summarizes your payment for the load and deductions for commission, advances (comp checks), etc.
- **Cost-Per-Mile-Calculation** —shows how much it costs you to drive a mile and will help you determine what loads to accept or reject.

Equipment records: Besides your financial records, you also have to keep accurate records for your equipment. You have to maintain the following documentation:

The identification of your vehicle, make, serial number, year, and tire size.

A schedule of that shows the type and due date of the various inspections and maintenance operations that have to be performed.

Records of actual inspection, repair or maintenance, and date and type.

Proof that lubrications were performed.

You must maintain these records for at least one full year. If you sell your truck, you must keep these records for at least another six months.

Establishing a routine will help you stay organized. Before you go on a trip, review your last inspection re- port and verify that all the noted repairs have been completed and that your truck is in proper operating condition.

When you come back from a trip, or at the end of your work day, complete a written vehicle inspection report, noting any repairs or work that needs to be performed so you can go back on the road with a safe vehicle that meets all requirements. You must keep a copy of the last vehicle report in the truck and every motor carrier must keep the original for at least three months.

Your trucking business must also have a safety rating from the United States Department of Transportation (DOT).

The Motor Carrier Safety Act of 1984 requires the Secretary of Transportation to determine the safety fitness of all motor carriers operating in interstate or foreign commerce.

You may obtain information about the safety ratings from the DOT's Public Information Office in Washington, DC, phone (202) 366- 5580, or your state's DOT office.

Accounts Payable: You will have to make regular monthly payments such as truck payments and insurance in addition to other bills you may receive. These billings are called "Accounts Payable."

Accounts Receivable: Every time you complete delivery of a load, money is owed to you. Your outstanding (unpaid) settlement checks are called "Accounts Receivable."

You have to keep track of these accounts because you need your income to pay your expenses. If you do not get paid on time, you cannot pay your bills on time. A simple method to maintain an overview of your financial obligations is using a monthly calendar where you record the individual amounts on their due dates.

Whenever you receive or make a payment, simply mark it off as shown on the sample calendar.

January 1, 2020	January 2, 2020	January 3, 2020
Day Off	Settle-ment	Truck payment
January 4, 2020	**January 5, 2020**	**January 6, 2020**
	Insurance	Tire bill

Cost-Per-Mile Calculation

You need to know two factors: (1) your operating expenses for a specific time period (a month, a calendar quarter, or a year) and (2) the miles driven in the corresponding time period.
For example if your quarterly operating expenses amount to

$15,205.00 and you have driven 22,194 miles in that quarter, your cost per mile is 69 cents. You can obtain these numbers from your monthly or quarterly financial

statements. Why is it important

to know your cost-per-mile factor?

Because it allows you to quickly

determine the profitability of a load.

Now that you have identified the operating cost, you start to think about ways to lower your cost and increase your profit margin. Keep in mind, if you have operated your truck only for a short time, the cost-per-mile factor may be misleading, because you do not yet have comparable historical data from previous years.

However, as a responsible business manager you should compare your cost-per-mile factor from month to month to determine how your business progresses.

Steps you can take to reduce operating expenses include:

- ☐ slow down and drive 60 miles per hour;
- ☐ use high quality, synthetic motor oil, and
- ☐ practice preventive maintenance.

You can realize savings of thousand dollars a year just by driving your truck at 60 mph. Engine manufacturers such as Volvo say, slowing down will (1) reduce fuel consumption, (2) reduce tire wear by as much as one fifth, and (3) extends the truck engine's life cycle, thus delaying the need for an engine overhaul. Study the following examples to see the dramatic difference: Assuming you drive **125,000** miles at **70 mph** with a fuel efficiency of **5.5** miles per gallon, your truck consumes **22,727** gallons of fuel. Assuming you drive **125,000** miles a year at **60 mph** with a fuel efficiency of **7** miles per gallon, your truck consumes **17,857** gallons of fuel. Slowing down will save **4,870** gallons of fuel, or **$12,905.50** at $2.65 per gallon of fuel.

Tire expenses constitute a significant part of your business budget and you have to replace worn tires to remain compliant with the law. You can extend the lifespan of your tires by driving carefully, avoiding speeding and proper tire maintenance.

Driving your truck at 60 mph can reduce tire wear by 20 percent. If your tire budget is $5,000 a year, you can save $1,000 a year by driving at 60 mph instead of 70 mph.

Three preventable problems cause premature tire wear. (1) **Improper inflation pressure** causes tires to run much hotter. An under-inflated tire will squirm and scrub the road surface much more than a properly inflated tire. The heat and friction combine to destroy a tire quickly. Therefore, keep the tires properly inflated.

Tire/Wheel Imbalance will cause a tire to hop off the road surface once for each revolution. With a tire turning between 400 and 600 rpm depending at speed, an out-of-balance steer tire hops off the road surface eight times a second, accumulating thousands of extra tire/road impacts a day. The best time to perform an on-vehicle balance check is at oil change time. (3) **Misalignment of any axle** causes tires to scuff along the road. If you run an average of 600 miles per day, the scuff results in rapid tire wear. To reduce tire wear, all rear axles must be aligned "straight ahead" within 1/32nd inch, all rear axles must be parallel within 1.32nd inch, and the steer axle toe-in must be accurate within 1/32nd inch.

A few basic maintenance procedures can increase tire mileage at least 30 percent. A new high quality steer tire costs approximately $425 and has a lifespan of 85,000 to 100,000 miles.

By implementing three maintenance steps, you can increase the life- span of your steer tires by 25,500 to 30,000 miles:

- ☐ check tire pressure frequently;
- ☐ make wheel balance a preventive maintenance procedure; and
- ☐ check alignment of all axles on your truck, including trailer, three times per year.

Registration & Taxes

Before you can legally operate your big rig in interstate commerce, you must:
- file Form 2290, Heavy Vehicle Use Tax, with the IRS,
- register the truck with IRP,
- register the truck with UCR, and
- register with IFTA.

Vehicle Registration. The Inter-modal Surface Transportation Act of 1991 created the **International Registration Plan (IRP)**, which is a streamlined system for truck registration and fuel tax reporting. Every state is a member of IRP, and your base (home) state's motor vehicle division is responsible for the licensing and registration of motor carriers under the IRP and the International Fuel Tax Agreement (IFTA).

Although you must register in every state you operate your truck, and each state collects vehicle registration fees and various taxes, under IRP you fill out one form indicating the states you will drive through and pay the registration fee to your base state. Only one license plate and one cab card is issued for each vehicle registered under IRP. The vehicle is known as an apportioned vehicle. Your cab card lists the states where your vehicle is apportioned. If you have to drive through a state where your truck is not registered, you can obtain a temporary registration.

In addition to IRP, you also need **Single State Registration System (SSRS)**, which is now replaced by **UCR**.

What is the UCR? The UCR (Unified Carrier Registration) is a program that replaced the (SSRS) Single State Registration System. The UCR Program requires individuals and companies that operate commercial motor vehicles in interstate or international commerce to register their business with a participating state and pay an annual fee based on the size of their fleet. This includes ALL carriers and truck owners, private, exempt, or for hire. Brokers, freight forwarders and leasing companies are also required to register and pay a fee unless they also operate as a motor carrier. Like SSRS, fees collected from the UCR system will be used by the states to support its safety

programs and US- DOT officer training. Unlike SSRS, the UCR system increases the number of fee-eligible transportation companies and its owned equipment, but lowers the fee per company. Kentucky, New Mexico, New York, and Oregon still require additional tax credentials.

Fuel & Road Taxes

The Heavy Duty Road Tax: Due on July 1st every year. If you fail to pay the tax on time, the IRS will assess penalties and late fees.

After the IRS has processed your Form 2290, you will receive a stamped copy for your records. Also keep the canceled check as proof of payment with your records.

The IRS provides Form 2290, Heavy Vehicle Use Tax Return, and it is self-explanatory. However, if you prefer, your accountant or a permit service can file the form for you.

The International Fuel Tax Agreement (IFTA) regulates the ad- ministration of road and fuel taxes among member jurisdictions. The purpose of **IFTA** is to establish and maintain the concept of one fuel use license and administering base jurisdiction for each licensee. A qualified motor vehicle is a motor vehicle used, designed, or maintained for transportation of persons or property and:

- Having two axles and a gross vehicle weight or registered gross vehicle weight exceeding 26,000 pounds; or
- Having three or more axles regardless of weight; or is used in combination, when such combination exceeds 26,000 pounds. Source: Arizona Motor Carrier Services.

The Owner-Operator (licensee) receives one fuel tax license, which is issued by the base state and authorizes travel in all IFTA jurisdictions. The IFTA license is valid for a calendar year, from January 1 to December 31, requiring annual renewals. You (the licensee) must file quarterly fuel tax returns reporting all miles accumulated by your truck in each jurisdiction (member state) to your base (home) state. The report must show all miles traveled and fuel purchased and consumed in each IFTA jurisdiction. Your base (home) jurisdiction will collect and transmit fees to other member jurisdictions or will issue a refund if you overpaid. Fuel tax audits are only performed by the base state.

Under this system, you must carefully plan and document your fuel usage and purchases and miles traveled in each state. For example, if you purchase 100 gallons of fuel but only use 50 in that jurisdiction, you are due a fuel tax credit. If you used 100 gallons but purchased only 50 gallons of fuel in that jurisdiction, you owe tax.

Log Books & Trip Sheets & ELD

The use of a "trip sheet" (see next page) can help you stay organized and compliant with IFTA regulations. If you use a computer in your business, consider fuel reporting software to document your fuel purchases and miles driven. A compliance services can handle the permit and fuel reporting process for you, if you prefer. These services charge monthly fees ranging from $30 to $60.

You can use a trucking compliance service for the following DOT requirements: Motor Carrier Authority (MC#) - Federal DOT # - Unified Carrier Registration (UCR) - IFTA fuel tax return - Random drug testing program - Heavy duty road tax - Driver files - Maintenance files - DOT auditing - fuel card program - finding the right ELD -

Some truckers only operate in one state, and if you are one of them, you may consider filing the quarterly fuel tax returns on your own, saving money.

You may obtain the complete International Fuel Tax Agreement, Administrative Procedures and Audit Guidelines, from your base state's department of transportation motor vehicles division. You can also obtain information online.

Log Book and Trip Sheets: Part 395 of the Federal Motor Carrier Safety Regulations outlines the **Hours of Service of Drivers** and recording requirements. The regulations state that "every driver who operates a commercial motor vehicle shall record his/ her duty status, in duplicate, for each 24-hour period." Generally, truckers use a log book to comply with this requirement. In this log, you must record your driving, on-duty and off-duty, and sleeper berth times as well as number of other details. You must keep this log current because regulatory agencies such as the DOT or highway patrol may request to inspect it at any time. You can obtain log books at truck stops.

After each trip, you also must complete a trip sheet where you record the date, state, route or highway, and loaded or empty miles. You will need this information to file your road and fuel tax reports. Owner-Operators must keep a copy of the FMCSR in their truck. The *Federal Motor Carrier Safety Regulations* pocketbook is published by J.J. Keller and Associates, and available at most truck stops. **All the above log book regulations are now outdated when the new ELD regulations became law on December 18, 2017.**

Electronic Logging Devices to be Required Across Commercial Truck and Bus Industries.

The U.S. Department of Transportation's Federal Motor Carrier Safety Administration (FMCSA) today announced the adoption of a Final Rule that will improve roadway safety by employing technology to strengthen commercial truck and bus drivers' compliance with hours-of-service regulations that prevent fatigue.

"Since 1938, complex, on-duty/off-duty logs for truck and bus drivers were made with pencil and paper, virtually impossible to verify," said U.S. Transportation Secretary Anthony Foxx. "This automated technology not only brings logging records into the modern age, it also allows roadside safety inspectors to unmask violations of federal law that put lives at risk."

The Final Rule requiring the use of electronic logging devices (ELD) will result in an annual net benefit of more than $1 billion – largely by reducing the amount of required industry paperwork. It will also increase the efficiency of roadside law enforcement personnel in reviewing driver records. Strict protections are included that will protect commercial drivers from harassment.

On an annual average basis, the ELD Final Rule is estimated to save 26 lives and prevent 562 injuries resulting from crashes involving large commercial motor vehicles.

"This is a win for all motorists on our nation's roadways," said FMCSA Acting Administrator Scott Darling. "Employing technology to ensure that commercial drivers comply with federal hours-of-service rules will prevent crashes and save lives."

An ELD automatically records driving time. It monitors engine hours, vehicle movement, miles driven, and location information.

Federal safety regulations limit the number of hours commercial drivers can be on-duty and still drive, as well as the number of hours spent driving. These limitations are designed to prevent truck and bus drivers from becoming fatigued while driving, and require that drivers take a work break and have a sufficient off-duty rest period before returning to on-duty status.

The four main elements of the ELD Final Rule include:

Requiring commercial truck and bus drivers who currently use paper log books to maintain hours-of-service records to adopt ELDs within two years. It is anticipated that approximately three million drivers will be impacted.

Strictly prohibiting commercial driver harassment. The Final Rule provides both procedural and technical provisions designed to protect commercial truck and bus drivers from harassment resulting from information generated by ELDs. [A separate FMCSA rulemaking further safeguards commercial drivers from being coerced to violate federal safety regulations and provides the agency with the authority to take enforcement actions not only against motor carriers, but also against shippers, receivers, and transportation intermediaries.]

- Setting technology specifications detailing performance and design requirements for ELDs so that manufacturers are able to produce compliant devices and systems – and purchasers are enabled to make informed decisions.

Establishing new hours-of-service supporting document (shipping documents, fuel purchase receipts, etc.) requirements that will result in additional paperwork reductions. In most cases, a motor carrier would not be required to retain supporting documents verifying on-duty driving time.

The ELD Final Rule permits the use of smart phones and other wireless devices as ELDs, so long as they satisfy technical specifications, are certified, and are listed on an FMCSA website. Canadian- and Mexican-domiciled drivers will also be required to use ELDs when operating on U.S. roadways.

Motor carriers who have previously installed compliant Automatic On-Board Recording Devices may continue to use the devices for an additional two years beyond the compliance date.

A copy of the ELD Final Rule announced today is available at: https://www.fmcsa.dot.gov/hours-service/elds/electronic-logging-devices-and-hours-service-supporting-documents.

Further information, including a comprehensive, searchable list of frequently asked questions, and a calendar of upcoming free training webinars, is available https://www.fmcsa.dot.gov/elds.

Our Information Package and Business Guide is based on experience and provides you with step-by-step information. We are sure it will be a valuable guide to help you start your own successful trucking business.

It explains the initial steps to become an Owner-Operator, the process of purchasing your own truck, and the lease-on process. Further, there is a financial section, information about fuel and road taxes, and details how to obtain your own operating authority.

Please study each step carefully. We are confident you soon will be a successful Owner-Operator.

Also, please remember to visit us on the Internet at www.truckingsuccess.com, where you will find additional useful services. The book itself can help you to make a decision, however, the process of becoming a business owner is much more complex, we offer therefore a consulting service.

Our web site now features a business plan including financial projections for entrepreneurs who would like to start a trucking company. Modified to your specifications, this sample business plan may be presented to apply for an SBA loan.

TruckingSuccess.com

7054 North 28th Drive
Phoenix, AZ 85051

Tel. (602) 864-8056

Email:
support@truckingsuccess.com

Information presented in this brochure is current at
the time of printing.
Specifications subject to change.
TX4-400-341
Copyright 2020 TruckingSuccess.com All
Rights Reserved.